The Up & Running Series from SYBEX

■ ■ ■ ■ ■ ■ ■ ■ ■

Other titles include Up & Running with:

- AutoSketch 3
- Carbon Copy Plus
- DOS 3.3
- Flight Simulator
- Harvard Graphics
- Lotus 1-2-3 Release 2.2
- Lotus 1-2-3 Release 3.1
- Norton Utilities
- PageMaker 4 on the PC
- PageMaker on the Macintosh
- PC Tools Deluxe 6
- PC-Write
- PROCOMM PLUS
- Q & A
- Quattro Pro 3
- Quicken 4
- ToolBook for Windows
- Turbo Pascal 5.5
- Windows 3.0
- Windows 286/386
- WordPerfect Library/Office PC
- XTreeGold 2
- Your Hard Disk

Up & Running with
WordPerfect ® 5.1

. . . .

Rita Belserene

SYBEX ®

San Francisco ■ Paris ■ Düsseldorf ■ Soest

Acquisitions Editor: Dianne King
Series Editor: Joanne Cuthbertson
Editor: Savitha Pichai
Technical Editor: Amelia S. Marshall
Word Processors: Lisa Mitchell, Ann Dunn, Scott Campbell
Series Designers: Ingrid Owen and Helen Bruno
Icon Designer: Helen Bruno
Screen Graphics: Cuong Le
Desktop Production Artist: Ingrid Owen
Proofreader: R. Marie Holmes
Indexer: Nancy Guenther
Cover Designer: Archer Design
Screen reproductions produced by XenoFont.

XenoFont is a trademark of XenoSoft.

SYBEX is a registered trademark of SYBEX, Inc.

TRADEMARKS: SYBEX has attempted throughout this book to distinguish propri-
etary trademarks from descriptive terms by following the capitalization style used by
the manufacturer.

SYBEX is not affiliated with any manufacturer.

Every effort has been made to supply complete and accurate information. However,
SYBEX assumes no responsibility for its use, nor for any infringement of the intel-
lectual property rights of third parties which would result from such use.

Library of Congress Card Number: 91-65241
ISBN: 0-89588-828-9

Manufactured in the United States of America
10 9 8 7 6 5 4 3 2

SYBEX Up & Running Books

■ ■ ■ ■ ■ ■ ■ ■ ■ ■

The Up & Running series of books from SYBEX has been developed for committed, eager PC users who would like to become familiar with a wide variety of programs and operations as quickly as possible. We assume that you are comfortable with your PC and that you know the basic functions of word processing, spreadsheets, and database management. With this background, Up & Running books will show you in 20 steps what particular products can do and how to use them.

Who this book is for

Up & Running books are designed to save you time and money. First, you can avoid purchase mistakes by previewing products before you buy them—exploring their features, strengths, and limitations. Second, once you decide to purchase a product, you can learn its basics quickly by following the 20 steps—even if you are a beginner.

What this book provides

The first step usually covers software installation in relation to hardware requirements. You'll learn whether the program can operate with your available hardware as well as various methods for starting the program. The second step often introduces the program's user interface. The remaining 18 steps demonstrate the program's basic functions, using examples and short descriptions.

Contents & structure

A clock shows the amount of time you can expect to spend at your computer for each step. Naturally, you'll need much less time if you only read through the step rather than complete it at your computer.

Special symbols and notes

You can also focus on particular points by scanning the short notes in the margins and locating the sections you are most interested in.

In addition, three symbols highlight particular sections of text:

The Action symbol highlights important steps that you will carry out.

The Tip symbol indicates a practical hint or special technique.

The Warning symbol alerts you to a potential problem and suggestions for avoiding it.

We have structured the Up & Running books so that the busy user spends little time studying documentation and is not burdened with unnecessary text. An Up & Running book cannot, of course, replace a lengthier book that contains advanced applications. However, you will get the information you need to put the program to practical use and to learn its basic functions in the shortest possible time.

We welcome your comments

SYBEX is very interested in your reactions to the Up & Running series. Your opinions and suggestions will help all of our readers, including yourself. Please send your comments to: SYBEX Editorial Department, 2021 Challenger Drive, Alameda, CA 94501.

Preface

WordPerfect has established itself as the industry standard for word processing programs. It is a remarkable program with an enormous array of powerful features. Version 5.1 includes everything that has already made WordPerfect such a popular program, plus some important new features. The most important changes include mouse support and the addition of pull-down menus as an option for giving commands.

This book is designed to give you the fastest possible introduction to WordPerfect, whether you are a newcomer to WordPerfect or have used earlier versions of the program. Throughout the book, concise instructions are given for using the traditional function-key techniques to give commands and also for using the newer pull-down menus.

Steps 1–13 cover basic, useful techniques. Steps 14–20 cover more advanced features that may or may not be applicable to your documents. These later steps are designed to be read in any order, so you can use them as the need arises.

Of course, no book of this length can cover all the features that are included with such a large program. Fortunately, WordPerfect provides you with extensive online help. This feature is covered in Step 2. You can use this online help to expand your knowledge of WordPerfect to include topics not covered here.

SYBEX also offers additional publications for readers who want to expand their knowledge of WordPerfect. *Mastering Word-Perfect 5.1* by Alan Simpson is a comprehensive introduction to all of WordPerfect's features. *Encyclopedia WordPerfect 5.1* by Greg Harvey and Kay Yarborough Nelson is a complete reference organized by practical functions, with business users in mind. *Desktop Publishing with WordPerfect 5.1* written by myself, Rita Belserene, is a guide to using WordPerfect's desktop publishing capabilities to create professional quality published documents. *WordPerfect 5.1 Tips and Tricks* by Alan R. Neibauer covers shortcuts and hints that can speed up your work. *The WordPerfect 5.1 Cookbook* by Alan Simpson and the accompanying diskette will help you create dozens of commonly used business and legal documents.

Let this book get you "up and running," and use online help or other references to add to your skill as the need arises.

Rita Belserene, April 1991

Table of Contents

Step 1
Installing
WordPerfect 5.1　1

Step 2
The User
Interface　5

Step 3
Basic Editing
Techniques　17

Step 4
Saving and
Retrieving Files　23

Step 5
Printing
Your Text　33

Step 6
Adding Text
Enhancements　41

Step 7
Revealing Formatting
Codes　47

Step 8
Working
with Margins　55

Step 9
Working
with Tabs　61

Step 10
Working with
Blocks of Text　69

Step 11
Using Search
and Replace　77

Step 12
Checking
Spelling　85

Step 13
Using the
Thesaurus　91

Step 14
Mutiple-Page
Documents　95

Step 15
Controlling
Hyphenation　103

Step 16
Creating
Columns　109

Step 17
Changing
Default Settings　117

Step 18
Macros and
Other Shortcuts　125

Step 19
Working
with Fonts　135

Step 20
Merging
Files　145

Installing
WordPerfect 5.1

Step 1 covers the use of the WordPerfect installation program and the setup required for using a mouse, which is an optional feature available with version 5.1 of WordPerfect. Before beginning the installation, you should check your hardware to ensure that your system is ready for you to proceed.

HARDWARE REQUIREMENTS
WordPerfect 5.1 requires the following hardware:

- An IBM or IBM-compatible computer running on MS-DOS version 2.0 or later. (You will need DOS version 3.0 or later if you are using high-density floppy drives.)

- At least 384K of available RAM.

Although a hard disk drive is not absolutely necessary, it is so strongly recommended that this book assumes you will be installing WordPerfect to a hard disk. To install the entire program, you will need:

- Approximately 4 megabytes (4000K) of available disk space.

If you have installed memory-resident programs in your system, you may need to remove these programs from memory before running the INSTALL program. This may require temporarily removing these programs from your AUTOEXEC.BAT file and then rebooting your system.

THE WORDPERFECT INSTALL PROGRAM

To install WordPerfect 5.1, all you need to do is run the INSTALL program that is provided with your WordPerfect program disks. (You cannot simply copy files directly from the distribution diskettes to your hard drive, as you may have done with earlier versions of WordPerfect or other software programs.) The INSTALL program expands the compressed archived program files, creates a directory on your hard disk for the files, and copies the files to that directory. If necessary, the INSTALL program can also update two standard system files, the CONFIG.SYS file and the AUTOEXEC.BAT file, to ensure that WordPerfect will run correctly on your system.

Installing WP on a hard disk

In order to run the INSTALL program:

1. Turn on your computer so that you are looking at a DOS prompt (for example, *C:\>*).

2. Place the diskette containing the INSTALL program in drive A.

3. Type

   `a:install`

and press Enter. At the *Continue? Yes (No)* prompt, press **Y** or Enter. This will initiate the installation program. Press Enter a second time to install to a hard disk.

4. Select Basic installation from the menu of installation choices by pressing either **1** or **B**.

In the next stages of the installation process, you will be asked which parts of the WordPerfect program you want to install. Each screen includes a brief summary of the function of the files you are about to install. As you proceed, the INSTALL program will prompt you when you need to change the disk in drive A until the entire program and its supporting files have been installed.

After the program files have been installed, the INSTALL program will ask you if want to modify the AUTOEXEC.BAT file to include the new WordPerfect directory in your system's search path. This modification allows you to start WordPerfect from any directory on your disk. WordPerfect 5.1 is automatically stored in the C:\WP51\ directory on a system using a hard disk.

Modifying the AUTO-EXEC.BAT file

The final steps of the INSTALL program allow you to select a printer (or printers) for use with WordPerfect. The list of printers is more than 30 screens long. Press **PgDn** until you see the appropriate model number. Type the number of the printer you want and press Enter. Then respond to any subsequent prompts to install the printer. After the printer has been installed, you will be returned to the operating system. (If you are using a color monitor, you might want to type **cls** and press Enter to clear your screen after you are returned to the operating system.) You are now ready to work with WordPerfect 5.1.

If you want to change any aspect of the installation, change to the C:\WP51 directory of your hard drive, type **install**, then press Enter. After you confirm the installation process, you will be moved directly to the printer installation sequence and you can proceed to select an additional printer or printers.

INSTALLING A MOUSE

Default mouse settings

WordPerfect supports the optional use of a mouse for selecting command options (covered in Step 2), cursor movement (covered in Step 3), and marking blocks of text (covered in Step 10). If you want to use a mouse, install it according to the instructions that come with your mouse. WordPerfect's default mouse settings are based on the assumption that you installed a *mouse driver* program, called MOUSE.COM, which provides instructions for the use of the mouse. If you want to use this default setting, the driver program must be run each time you turn on your computer and *before* you run WordPerfect. This can be handled automatically by modifying your AUTOEXEC.BAT program so that the driver program is run each time you turn on the computer. (The cost in memory overhead used may not justify this automatic operation unless you use the mouse for other purposes as well.) Alternatively, you can type the command that runs the mouse (for example, type **mouse**, then press Enter) before you start WordPerfect.

The mouse menu

In addition to supporting the use of a mouse driver, WordPerfect supports a variety of mouse types that are listed in a Mouse Type menu. If your mouse is listed on this menu, and if you don't use a mouse for other programs, you may want to select this option. Once you have selected a mouse type this way, you do not need to run the MOUSE.COM program each time you want to work with WordPerfect. To select a mouse type from the Mouse Type menu, use the WordPerfect Set-up menu covered in Step 17 of this book.

The User Interface

This Step uses a tutorial approach to introduce you to the Word-Perfect interface. As you work, you will learn how to start WordPerfect; how to interpret the information that appears on screen; how to give commands using either one of two available methods (the keyboard function keys or WordPerfect's pull-down menus); and how to exit WordPerfect. You will also learn how to use the online help feature to get quick answers to questions you have about working with WordPerfect 5.1.

CREATING A DIRECTORY FOR YOUR FILES

Before you start WordPerfect, use the directions that follow to create a directory called PRACTICE to store the work you do in the tutorial sections of this book.

1. Turn on the computer so that you are looking at the DOS prompt (for example, *C:\>*).

2. Type

    `md\practice`

    then press Enter to create the PRACTICE directory.

(Do not change to this directory yet. You will learn how to change directories from within WordPerfect in a later exercise.)

STARTING WORDPERFECT

To start WordPerfect, at the DOS prompt type the command

`wp`

and press Enter. (If you did not put WordPerfect in your system's search path when you installed the program, you must change to the WordPerfect directory by typing **cd\wp51** before you type **wp** to start the program.)

Your initial view of WordPerfect will be an empty document screen like the one shown in Figure 2.1. The bottom of this screen is known as the *status line*. WordPerfect uses the status line to display important information about your document and to present a variety of questions, or *prompts,* that you will need to respond to as you work with WordPerfect.

THE WORDPERFECT STATUS LINE

The right-hand side of the status line provides you with information about the editing cursor. There are four items in this section of the status line.

Identifying the cursor location

The *Doc* item identifies the current document screen. WordPerfect allows you to work with two separate documents simultaneously. These are identified as *Doc 1* and *Doc 2* in the status line. When

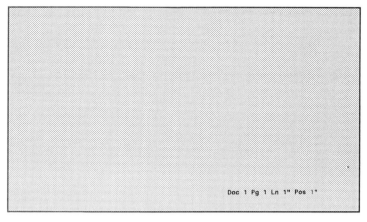

Doc 1 Pg 1 Ln 1" Pos 1"

- *Figure 2.1: An empty WordPerfect document screen*

you first start WordPerfect, it is ready for you to work with Document 1. You will learn how to use Document 2 in Step 4 of this book. (If you are working in WordPerfect and your work seems to vanish, check the Doc indicator before you panic to see if you have inadvertently changed from Document 1 to Document 2.)

The *Pg* indicator identifies the page number for the current cursor location.

The *Ln* indicator identifies the vertical position of the cursor with respect to the final printed page of text. When you first install WordPerfect, the line indicator is set to a default of 1". This means that the first line of text will be printed one inch from the top edge of the printed page. (You will learn how to change the default settings for margins in Step 8.)

The *Pos* (position) indicator marks the horizontal location of the cursor as measured from the left edge of the printed page. The default setting for the left-hand margin is 1".

**Caps Lock
and
Num Lock**

The *Pos* indicator serves an additional function; the letters *Pos* change appearance to indicate two important keyboard settings. If the position indicator is flashing, it means that the Num Lock key is engaged. When this key is engaged, the numeric keypad can be used for typing numbers. When it is not engaged, the same keypad can be used for moving the cursor. (The default setting for the Num Lock key depends on the system you are using.)

The *Pos* indicator also changes appearance when you engage the Caps Lock key. When this key is engaged, the position indicator is displayed in all uppercase letters.

CHOOSING BETWEEN THE FUNCTION KEYS AND PULL-DOWN MENUS

WordPerfect 5.1 provides you with a choice of two methods for giving commands: the function keys (F1, F2, F3, and so forth) and pull-down menus. You can use either technique alone, or work with a combination of the two. (If you have used earlier versions of WordPerfect, you will be familiar with most of the function key commands for version 5.1.)

Using the Function Keys

Your keyboard has either 10 or 12 function keys, depending on its design. Function keys F11 and F12 are optional keys with WordPerfect 5.1. Each function key can be used to give four different commands, depending on whether it is pressed alone, or in combination with the Ctrl, Shift, or Alt key.

Try the following:

1. Hold down the Shift key and then touch F7. This command (Shift-F7) is used for printing. You should see a

menu of print options appear. (These options will be covered in Step 5.)

2. To cancel this print command, press F1. Use this key to cancel any incomplete command, such as the print command you just gave. The document screen should reappear.

Pressing F1 to cancel a command

Using Pull-Down Menus

To work with pull-down menus, you must first display the pull-down menu bar shown in Figure 2.2. This can be done either with a mouse or from the keyboard.

To use pull-down menus with the keyboard, press Alt-= to open the menu bar. This displays the name of the nine pull-down menus. (Repeat the Alt-= command or press F1 to turn off the menu bar display.) To see the list of options available with a pull-down menu, you can use the arrow keys to highlight the menu heading and then press Enter to open the menu under that heading.

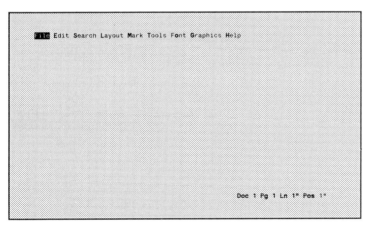

File Edit Search Layout Mark Tools Font Graphics Help

Doc 1 Pg 1 Ln 1" Pos 1"

■ *Figure 2.2: The pull-down menu bar*

Alternatively, you can press the highlighted letter in any menu heading (without pressing Enter) to open the menu under that heading. Once a menu is opened, you can select a command from any of the menu choices using either of the two techniques just described. These command choices will lead you eventually to the same WordPerfect menus that are displayed when you use the function keys.

Try the following:

1. Press Alt-= to open the menu bar.

2. Press Enter to open the File menu (which is already highlighted).

3. Press **P** to select the Print command. This displays the same WordPerfect menu you saw by pressing Shift-F7.

4. Press F1 to cancel the command and return to the document screen.

WORKING WITH A MOUSE

The use of a mouse for giving commands is an optional feature that is new with version 5.1. When your mouse is properly installed, a small rectangular *mouse cursor* becomes visible as soon as you move the mouse on your work surface. Techniques for selecting command options using a mouse are summarized in Table 2.1. Notice that the action of the mouse button depends on what is on screen when that button is clicked. If a document is on screen, the right button opens the pull-down menu bar; if a menu is on screen, the right button closes the menu and returns you to the document screen; and if a status line prompt is on screen, the right mouse button acts like the Enter key, accepting the default response choice. The left button is used to select menu options if a menu is on screen, but can also be used to move the cursor (see Step 3) or mark a block of text (see Step 10) when a document is on screen.

In order to:	Use the mouse as follows:
Display the pull-down menu bar	Click the *right* mouse button.
Select a menu item	Move the mouse cursor to the item you want and click the *left* mouse button.
Close a WordPerfect menu	Click the *right* mouse button.
Accept the default response to a status line prompt (equivalent to pressing Enter)	Click the *right* mouse button, or double-click the *left* mouse button.
Cancel a command	Click the *middle* mouse button. (With a two-button mouse, hold either button down and click the other.)

Table 2.1: Using a Mouse with WordPerfect Menus

If you have installed a mouse, try the following:

Using a
mouse with
pull-down
menus

1. Move the mouse on your work surface and locate the rectangular mouse cursor.

2. Click the right mouse button to open the menu bar.

3. Move the *mouse cursor* to any position on the File heading and then click the left mouse button to open the File menu.

4. Move the mouse cursor to the word Print and click the left mouse button to open the Print menu.

5. Click the right mouse button to close the menu. The document screen should reappear.

WORKING WITH WORDPERFECT MENUS

Making menu selections

Working with WordPerfect involves many menus such as the Print menu you just displayed. You can use either the keyboard or a mouse to make choices from these menus. To make selections with the keyboard, press either the highlighted number or letter to select a menu option. To make selections with a mouse, move the mouse cursor to the selection you want and press the left mouse button.

Closing menus

To exit from a WordPerfect menu using the keyboard, press F7, the Spacebar, or Enter. (With some menus, not all three options are available.) To exit from a menu with the mouse, click the right mouse button. All of these exit options save any changes you have made to a document with a menu. Press F1 to close a menu *without* saving changes.

You will have an opportunity to work with a WordPerfect menu when you change directories in the next exercise.

CHANGING DIRECTORIES

If WordPerfect is in your system's search path, you can change to any directory before you start the program, and WordPerfect will continue to work in that directory until you select a new default directory. One way to change directories from within WordPerfect is by using the Other Directory option of the List Files command as follows:

1. Press F5 (or open the Files menu and select List Files). The left side of the status line should now identify the directory you were working in when you started WordPerfect.

2. Press Enter to display the List Files screen.

3. Press **7** or **O** (or use a mouse) to select Other Directory from the menu on the bottom of this screen. On the status line, WordPerfect will display the words *New Directory* followed by the current directory path.

4. Type the new directory path exactly as it appears below. (As soon as you start to type, the current directory display will disappear automatically.)

    `c:\practice`

5. Press Enter. The display on the status line should now read:

    `C:\PRACTICE\*.*`

6. Press Enter to list the files in this directory. (The list will be empty because you haven't yet placed any files in this directory.)

7. Press the Spacebar or the F7 key, or click the right mouse button to return to the document screen.

USING ONLINE HELP

WordPerfect's online help feature provides you with quick, easy access to information about all of the features provided with the program. This information is organized both alphabetically and by keystroke. To use the online help, either press F3 or display the pull-down menu bar, open the Help menu, and then select Help. You can locate information about WordPerfect in either of the following ways, mixing the two approaches during a sequence of menu displays if you wish.

Using F3 to access online help

■ Press any letter of the alphabet to see an alphabetical list of commands beginning with that letter. (Press the letter again to see more options if the list is too long to fit on screen.)

■ Press any function key combination to learn about what that key combination accomplishes. (Each function key combination is given a name that appears under the heading *WordPerfect Key* in the alphabetical command listings.)

When you see a menu display while you are using the online help, you can learn more about any item on that menu by pressing the highlighted number or letter that corresponds to that menu choice.

Using Enter or the Spacebar to exit from help

As long as you are still working with online help, pressing a key gives you information about that key, but does not actually execute a command. In order to execute commands or continue work on a document, you must exit from online help. Press Enter or use the Spacebar to exit from online help and return to the document screen.

The following exercise illustrates how to work with online help:

1. Press F3 to enter online help. Read the information that appears on screen about how to use this feature.

2. Press **P** to display a list of commands beginning with that letter. Press **P** again to see more items on this list and to find the Print command.

3. Press Shift-F7 to display the options in the print menu, then press **V** to learn more about the View Document feature.

4. Press F1 to learn more about the Cancel command.

5. Continue to explore the help menu by pressing either letters or function keys.

6. Press the Spacebar when you want to return to the document screen.

EXITING FROM WORDPERFECT

Use the Exit command to exit from WordPerfect. To initiate this command with the keyboard, press F7. To use the pull-down menus, open the File menu and select Exit. WordPerfect will respond with a series of prompts that you must respond to before exiting. (These prompts can be used to save documents and/or clear the document screen. These techniques are covered in Step 4 of this book.)

Pressing
F7 to exit

To exit from WordPerfect without saving the work you have on screen:

1. Press F7 (or open the File menu and select Exit). Word-Perfect will display the following prompt on the status line:

   Save document? Yes (No)

2. Press **N** (or move the mouse cursor to No and click the left mouse button). The next status line prompt reads:

   Exit WP? No (Yes)

3. Press **Y** (or use the mouse to select Yes).

You should always exit from WordPerfect before turning off your computer. If power is interrupted before you exit from Word-Perfect, you will see the following prompt the next time you try to start the program:

```
Are other copies of WordPerfect currently
running? (Y/N)
```

Press **N** in response to this question to display the WordPerfect document screen.

Basic Editing
Techniques

■ ■ ■ ■ ■ ■ ■ ■ ■ ■

This Step summarizes basic techniques for creating and editing
documents in WordPerfect. You will learn how to move the cursor
efficiently through your document using either the keyboard or a
mouse, and how to insert and delete short sections of text.

SOFT AND HARD RETURNS

WordPerfect allows you to type text without having to press a carriage return (Enter) at the end of each line. When WordPerfect
starts a new line for you, the division between lines is known as a
soft return. If you edit a document containing soft returns in a way
that affects the number of characters on a line, the lines are automatically readjusted for you as soon as you move the cursor.

When you start a new line by pressing Enter, you put a *hard
return* between lines. WordPerfect will always start a new line
where you have entered a hard return, regardless of any subsequent editing changes.

MOVING THE CURSOR

In order to review and edit your documents, you need to move the cursor through existing text. This can be done using either the keyboard or a mouse.

Keyboard Cursor Control Commands

It is possible to move the cursor anywhere in a document simply by using the four arrow keys ($\uparrow$, $\downarrow$, $\rightarrow$, $\leftarrow$); however, this is an inefficient way to work. WordPerfect offers a variety of cursor control commands that allow you to get quickly to the part of a document you want to view and/or edit. These commands are summarized in Table 3.1. (These cursor control commands can only move the cursor through existing text; the cursor will move neither below the last line of text nor to the right of the last character in a line.)

Keystroke	Effect
$\leftarrow$	Right one character.
$\rightarrow$	Left one character.
$\uparrow$	Up one line.
$\downarrow$	Down one line.
Ctrl-$\rightarrow$	Right one word.
Ctrl-$\leftarrow$	Left one word.
Home,$\leftarrow$	Beginning of current line on screen.
Home,$\rightarrow$	End of current line on screen.
End	End of current line (even if it extends beyond the screen).

Table 3.1: Cursor Control Commands

Keystroke	Effect
Home,Home,↑	Beginning of document.
Home,Home,↓	End of document.
Home,↑ *or* +	Top of current screen, then top of previous screen.
Home,↓ *or* −	Bottom of current screen, then bottom of next screen.
Page Up (PgUp)	First line of previous page.
Page Down (PgDn)	First line of next page.
Ctrl-Home	Move to specified page. (Enter page number at *Go to* prompt on status line.)

Table 3.1: Cursor Control Commands (cont.)

Some commands involve using two keys simultaneously. As you can see in the table, these are written with a hyphen between the key names (for example, Ctrl-←). Others involve pressing keys in *sequence,* and when this is the case, the key names are separated by commas (for example Home, →).

Using keys in sequence or simultaneously

The term *scrolling* describes the process of viewing different sections of a document that is too long to see on screen at one time. You can scroll either screen by screen, or page by page. The word *screen* is used to describe the text that is visible on your monitor screen at any given time. The word *page* is used to describe the amount of text that will fit on a single printed page.

Scrolling terms

You can scroll from screen to screen by using the + and − keys located on the *numeric keypad* if Num Lock is disengaged. (The + and − keys along the top of the keyboard enter those symbols into the text you are typing, as do the + and − keys on the numeric

Using Keypad + and Keypad −

keypad when Num Lock is engaged.) Use Page Up (PgUp) and Page Down (PgDn) to scroll from page to page.

In order to practice the cursor control commands, start Word-Perfect, and type a short paragraph of text. Use this text to practice using the first eleven cursor commands in Table 3.1. The last five commands in the table are useful only with longer documents. As you begin to create multiple page documents, return to this table to acquaint yourself with these additional cursor controls.

Using a Mouse to Control the Cursor

WordPerfect 5.1 also supports the use of a mouse for cursor control. To move the editing cursor (the small flashing line), move the mouse cursor to the desired location, then click the *left* mouse button. To scroll to parts of the document that are not visible on the current screen, move the mouse cursor to the top or bottom of the screen, then hold down the *right* mouse button while you continue to move the mouse in the desired direction.

DELETING TEXT

The simplest way to delete text is to use the Delete (Del key), which deletes the character at the cursor location. If you hold the Delete key down, WordPerfect will continue to delete subsequent characters. In addition to this basic technique, WordPerfect provides a variety of commands to make your work more efficient. Commands for deleting text are summarized in Table 3.2. Additional techniques for deleting larger blocks of text are covered in Step 10.

Keystroke	Effect
Delete (Del)	Delete character at the cursor.
Backspace	Delete character to left of cursor
Ctrl-Backspace	Delete entire word.
Home, Backspace	Delete from cursor to beginning of word.
Home, Delete	Delete from cursor to end of word.
Ctrl-End	Delete from cursor to end of line.
Ctrl-Page Down	Delete from cursor to end of current page. (You must confirm this by pressing **Y** after giving the command.)

Table 3.2: Commands for Deleting Text

If you inadvertently delete text that you meant to keep, you can restore it by using the Cancel command (F1), or by opening the Edit menu and selecting Undelete. When you do this, WordPerfect temporarily inserts the text of your most recent deletion using reverse video and displays the following menu on the status line:

Restoring deleted text

Undelete: 1 Restore; 2 Previous Deletion

Select Restore if you want to insert the deleted material back into your text at the current cursor position. Select Previous Deletion to see the next-to-last deletion. Press **2** or ↓ repeatedly to see the last three deletions. Then press **1** to select the one you want inserted at the cursor location. WordPerfect stores your most recent three deletions. Deletions you made prior to this cannot be restored. To return to your text without inserting any deleted material, press F1, Enter, or the Spacebar, or click the right mouse button.

Notice that the Cancel key (F1) has two functions. If a WordPerfect menu is displayed, this key closes the menu without

The two uses of the Cancel command

Basic Editing Techniques **21**

saving any changes you have made. If your document is on screen, this key is used to undelete text.

INSERTING ADDITIONAL TEXT

Insert and typeover modes

WordPerfect allows you to work in two modes, *insert* mode and *typeover* mode. In insert mode, anything you type is inserted immediately to the left of the current cursor position. The remaining text is moved to the right in order to make room for each new character as it is inserted. In typeover mode, each new character you type replaces the existing character at the cursor position. As you continue to type, existing text is continually replaced by new text.

Use the Insert (or Ins) key to choose between insert and typeover modes. When you first start WordPerfect, it is ready to work in insert mode. To change to typeover mode, press the Insert key. The word *Typeover* will appear in the lower-left portion of the status line to indicate that you are now in typeover mode. Pressing the Insert key again removes the word Typeover from the status line and returns you to insert mode. For most word processing applications, it is quicker and easier to work in insert mode. Commands for deleting text behave identically whether you are in insert or typeover mode.

Use the sample text you have created to practice deleting and inserting text. When you are done, exit from WordPerfect without saving your work (F7, N, N).

Saving and Retrieving Files

■ ■ ■ ■ ■ ■ ■ ■ ■ ■ ■

In this Step, you will learn the essentials of saving and retrieving your document files. You will also learn how to work with different directories on your hard disk, how to make back up copies of hard disk files to a floppy disk, how to combine documents, and how to work with two files simultaneously.

SAVING AND NAMING
A FILE THE FIRST TIME

To initiate the save procedure, either press F10 or open the File menu and select Save. When a file has not yet been saved, this brings the following prompt to the status line:

`Document to be saved:`

At this prompt, type in any valid file name and press Enter. Once you have saved a file and given it a name, that name will appear in the lower-left portion of the status line preceded by the drive

Identifying
a file's
location

and/or directory that the file is located in (known as the document *path*). For example, if you are working from the A drive and save a file using the name SMITH.LTR, the status line will read *A:\SMITH.LTR*. If you save a file of the same name while working in a subdirectory of the C drive called LETTERS, the status line will read *C:\LETTERS\SMITH.LTR*.

To practice saving a file, start WordPerfect and change to the PRACTICE directory (press F5, Enter, then **7**, and then type the directory and path; or see Step 2), then proceed as follows:

1. Type the following:

   This is the first line of my sample
   document.

2. Press F10 (or open the File menu and select Save).

3. In response to the *Document to be saved:* prompt, type:

   sample

   and press Enter.

4. Notice that the following file identification has appeared on the status line:

   C:\PRACTICE\SAMPLE

Leave this document on screen. You will use it in the next section to learn how to save an updated file.

SAVING AN UPDATED FILE

Replacing existing files

After a file has been saved, whenever you initiate a Save command the *Document to be saved:* prompt will automatically be followed by the path and document name that have been assigned to that document. If you simply want to update an existing document without changing its name or location, press Enter in response to this prompt. This will bring up a prompt that asks you if you want to replace the existing file. Although the default response to this prompt is No, under most circumstances you will want to respond by selecting Yes. When you select Yes, WordPerfect replaces the file that you previously saved with the updated version of the file as you see it on the monitor screen.

Add a second line of text to the SAMPLE file you just created. To save the updated version of the file:

1. Press F10 (or open the File menu and select Save). The following prompt will appear on the status line:

    `Document to be saved: C:\PRACTICE\SAMPLE`

2. Press Enter (or click the right mouse button). The prompt will change to read:

    `Replace C:\PRACTICE\SAMPLE? No (Yes)`

3. Press **Y** (or use the mouse cursor to select Yes).

There are several additional options you might want to use when you see the *Document to be saved:* prompt followed by the existing file path and name. You can type a new file name rather than press Enter to accept the existing name. (As soon as you press a character, the old name and path will disappear.) Doing this creates two separate files—the original, unedited file and the updated version with the new file name. You can also edit the existing file name and/or path by moving the cursor through the file name display and then deleting and/or inserting characters. (Once you have moved the cursor, the old path and file name will not disappear when you type additional characters.) This also results in two separate files. These files may have different names, or the same name and two different locations.

SAVING AS YOU EXIT

WordPerfect also allows you to combine saving a file with exiting from WordPerfect. When you press F7, or select Exit from the File menu, the first prompt that appears reads:

Save document? Yes (No)

If you select Yes, WordPerfect responds with the save prompts described above. If you have not made any changes to a document since the last time you saved it, you will also see the following display on the right side of the status line:

(Text was not modified)

This message tells you that you have not changed your text in any way since the last time you saved it. When this message appears, there is no need to repeat the save procedure.

CLEARING THE SCREEN

If you want to edit another document without exiting from WordPerfect, you must first clear the document screen. This is true whether you want to type a new document or retrieve one that you have already typed and saved. WordPerfect *does not* automatically clear an existing document when you retrieve a file. Clearing the screen is identical to exiting from WordPerfect except for the final step. Initiate the process by pressing F7 (or selecting Exit from the File menu), then respond to the save prompts as they appear. The final prompt reads:

Exit WP? No (Yes)

Select No in response to this prompt when you want to clear the existing text from the document screen without exiting from WordPerfect.

To clear the SAMPLE document from your screen:

1. Press F7 (or open the File menu and select Exit). You will see the *Save document?* prompt on the left side of the status line and (unless you have made changes to this document since the last exercise) the message *(Text was not modified)* on the right.

2. Press **N** to skip the save procedure.

3. Press **N** again in response to the *Exit WP?* prompt to clear the screen without exiting from WordPerfect.

RETRIEVING FILES

Once a file has been saved, you can retrieve it with either the Retrieve command or the List Files command.

The Retrieve Command

To use the Retrieve command, you must remember the exact name of the file you want to retrieve. To initiate this command, either press Shift-F10, or open the File menu and select Retrieve. This will result in the following prompt on the status line:

`Document to be retrieved:`

In response to this prompt, type the name of the document you want to retrieve and press Enter. This will bring the file you named into the document screen.

Be sure to clear the document screen before retrieving a new file. If the screen is not clear, the new file will be added to the existing file at the current cursor location.

The List Files Command

A more flexible and useful way to retrieve files is with the List Files command. To initiate this command, press F5 or open the File menu and select List Files. WordPerfect responds to the List Files command by displaying the current directory path on the left-hand portion of the status line. Press Enter to display the List Files screen. This screen contains an alphabetical list of the files in the current directory and a menu of file management options. A sample List Files screen is shown in Figure 4.1.

Retrieving a File from the Files List

To retrieve a file from the List Files screen, highlight the file you want to retrieve, then select *Retrieve* by pressing 1 or R (or by moving the mouse cursor to *Retrieve* and clicking the left mouse button).

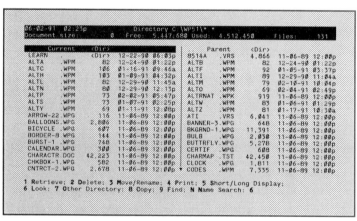

■ *Figure 4.1: The List Files screen*

Notice that you do not retrieve a file simply by pressing Enter after you highlight the file name. If you do press Enter, WordPerfect will show you that document, but you will not be able to edit it in any way.

To retrieve the SAMPLE file you created earlier:

1. Begin with a clear document screen. If you have practice work on screen, clear it by using the Exit command (F7, N, N).

2. Press F5 (or open the Files menu and select List Files). The lower-left portion of your screen should read:

   Dir C:\PRACTICE*.*

3. Press Enter (or click the right button) to confirm that this is the directory listing you want to view.

4. Highlight the SAMPLE file by moving the cursor using the arrow keys.

5. Select Retrieve (by pressing **1** or **R** or by using the mouse) to retrieve the file.

Combining Files

If there is a document on screen when you retrieve a file with the List Files command, you will see the prompt

Retrieve into current document? No (Yes)

after you have selected the Retrieve option. Respond Yes to this prompt if you want to combine the document you selected from the files list with the document that is currently on screen. When you do this, the document file you retrieve is inserted into the document on screen at the current cursor location.

If you see this prompt and you are not trying to combine documents, press N or Enter to return to the files list, then return to the document screen (by pressing the Spacebar or clicking the right mouse button) and clear the screen (F7, N, N) before trying to retrieve the file.

Choosing a Directory and Specifying Files

You can use the status line prompt that appears when you first invoke the List Files command to change directories and/or specify particular files that you want to view in the files directory. This prompt shows the current directory on the left-hand side of the status line.

You can respond to this prompt in one of the following ways:

Changing directories

- Enter a new directory path or edit the existing path to see a list of files in a different directory without changing the default directory. (This means that subsequent Save and List Files commands will work with the original directory.)

- Press =, then enter a new directory path or edit the existing path to list the files in a new directory *and* change that to the default directory. (This means that subsequent Save and List Files commands will work with the new directory.)

Listing selected files

- Edit the *.* using standard DOS rules for listing files to select only certain files for the list. (For example, *.WPG will list only files with the .WPG extension and R*.* will list all files starting with the letter R.)

After you have edited the file name and/or directory path, press Enter to display the List Files screen that reflects these changes.

MAKING AND RETRIEVING BACK-UP COPIES

It is a good idea to have copies of any important files on floppy disks as well as on your hard drive. The Copy feature of the List Files screen can be used for this purpose. When you use this feature, WordPerfect copies the file you have highlighted to any disk or directory you specify.

To copy the SAMPLE file to drive A, place a formatted disk in the A drive and then proceed as follows:

Saving to the A drive

1. Display the List Files screen (F5, Enter) and highlight the SAMPLE file.

2. Select Copy from the menu at the bottom of this screen.

3. Type

    A:

    then press Enter to copy the file to the A drive.

4. Press the Spacebar or click the right mouse button to return to the document screen.

(If there is already a file by the same name on the disk in drive A, you will be prompted to confirm that you want to replace the existing file.)

Copying multiple files

WordPerfect also allows you to copy many files simultaneously. To do this, display the List Files Screen, then highlight each file you want to copy and press * to mark the files with an asterisk. (Press * again to remove the mark.) Once the files are marked, select Copy from the List Files menu. WordPerfect will respond with a series of prompts that allow you to specify a new name and/or destination for the duplicate files.

STEP

4

*Retrieving
backup
files*

To retrieve a file from the A drive, you need to change to the A drive either by editing the file path when you first invoke the List Files command or by using the Other Directory feature of the List Files screen.

WORKING WITH TWO DOCUMENTS

WordPerfect allows you to work with two documents simultaneously. This can be useful when you want to use one document as reference, or want to combine documents using the block editing techniques that are covered in Step 10. To switch back and forth between documents, press Shift-F3 or open the Edit menu and select Switch Document.

When you are working with two documents, you must use the Exit command to exit from each document separately before you can exit from WordPerfect. It does not matter which document you exit from first.

Printing Your Text

In this Step, you will learn two methods of printing documents in WordPerfect: printing directly from the on-screen display and printing from the List Files screen. Options for printing selected pages, controlling the number of printed copies, and adjusting the quality of printed output are also covered. Finally, you will learn how to use WordPerfect's View Document feature in order to preview how your documents will look on the printed page.

PRINTING FROM THE DOCUMENT SCREEN

To invoke the WordPerfect Print command, either press Shift-F7 or open the File menu and select Print. This command displays the Print menu shown in Figure 5.1. When you select the Full Document option from this menu, WordPerfect prints the entire document that you are currently working with. You do not need to save a document in order to use this command, and it does not matter where the cursor is located. WordPerfect prints the document as it appears on screen.

```
Print

    1 - Full Document
    2 - Page
    3 - Document on Disk
    4 - Control Printer
    5 - Multiple Pages
    6 - View Document
    7 - Initialize Printer


Options

    S - Select Printer              HP LaserJet III
    B - Binding Offset              0"
    N - Number of Copies            1
    U - Multiple Copies Generated by  WordPerfect
    G - Graphics Quality            Medium
    T - Text Quality                High



Selection: 0
```

■ *Figure 5.1: The Print menu*

Print a sample document as directed below:

1. Start WordPerfect, change to the PRACTICE directory, and be sure you are looking at a clear document screen.

2. Type this sentence:

   ```
   This is a printer test.
   ```

3. Press Shift-F7 (or open the File menu and select Print). This will display the Print menu.

4. Press **1** or **F** (or use the mouse) to select Full Document. Your document will be printed and you will be returned to the document screen. Leave the document on screen for the next exercise.

PRINTING FROM THE LIST FILES SCREEN

You can also print files by using the Print option on the List Files screen. When you use this printing technique, WordPerfect prints documents that have been saved to the disk. You can print any saved document or documents with this command regardless of what is currently visible in the document screen. When you use this printing option, WordPerfect prompts you to specify which pages you want to print. The default option is to print the entire document. (See "Printing Selected Pages" below for more information about this feature.)

To print the SAMPLE document that you created in Step 4, without changing the current document display:

1. Display the List Files screen for the PRACTICE directory (F5, Enter).

2. Highlight the SAMPLE document.

3. Press **4** or **P** (or use the mouse) to select Print from the menu at the bottom of the screen. You should see the following prompt at the bottom of your screen:

   `Page(s): (All)`

4. Press Enter or click the right mouse button to accept this default option. Your document will be printed and the List Files screen will remain visible.

5. Press the Spacebar or click the right mouse button to return to the document screen.

By marking files with an asterisk, you can print more than one file with a single print command. When you do this, WordPerfect will prompt you to confirm that you want to print all marked files.

USING THE VIEW DOCUMENT FEATURE

The WordPerfect document screen does not show you how your pages will actually look when they are printed. The View Document option of the Print menu is designed to let you preview a facsimile of the printed page. To use this feature, press Shift-F7 or select Print from the File menu, then select the View Document feature. WordPerfect responds with a graphic display of what your document will look like when it is printed. When the entire document is not visible in this initial display, you can use Word-Perfect's cursor control options to view different parts of the document on screen. A sample View Document screen containing a short business letter is shown in Figure 5.2.

View Document options

A menu of choices at the bottom of the View Document screen allows you to decide how much of the document you want to view. Option 1 (100%) magnifies the document to the approximate size it will be when printed. With this magnification, you may be able to read the text (depending on your monitor), but you cannot see an entire page of text. Option 2 (200%) increases the magnification, showing more detail, but less text. Option 3 (Full Page)

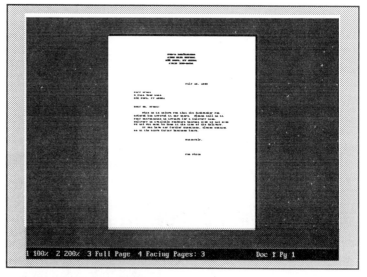

■ *Figure 5.2: The View Document screen*

shows you an entire page of text. (This is the default option, which was used to create Figure 5.2.) Although you cannot read the text at this magnification, it is useful for adjusting overall page layout. Option 4 (Facing Pages) is for use with multiple-page documents. This option shows you two pages at a time, placing even numbered pages on the left, as they appear in bound documents.

When you select a View Document option, WordPerfect returns to that same magnification each time you use the View Document feature until you change the setting again.

To view the printer test document currently on screen:

1. Press Shift-F7 (or open the File menu and select Print). This will open the Print menu.

2. Press **6** or **V** (or use the mouse) to select View Document.

3. Press **1**, then **2** to view the document at different magnifications, then press **3** to return to the Full Page option. (If you are using a mouse, you can select view options by using the mouse to move the arrow pointer to the option you want, and then clicking the left mouse button.)

4. Press the Spacebar (or click the right mouse button) to return to the document screen.

5. Clear the screen without saving the document (F7, N, N).

PRINTER CONTROL OPTIONS

WordPerfect's printer control options allow you to print multiple copies of a document, print selected pages, and control the quality of your printed output.

Printing Multiple Copies

To print more than one copy of a document, open the Print menu and select Number of Copies. When you do this, the cursor will move to the number located to the right of this option (ordinarily 1). Type the number of copies you want to have printed, then press Enter. If you save a document after you change the Number of Copies option, WordPerfect will store the value you entered and print that number of copies each time you print the document, until you reset the value.

Printing Selected Pages

If you work with longer documents, you may not always want to print an entire document. To print selected pages, either use the List Files screen to print your document, or open the Print menu and select the Multiple Pages option. Both of these two options present you with the following prompt:

`Page(s):`

(If you use the List Files screen, this prompt will be followed by a default response for printing all the pages.)

To print selected pages from the document, respond to this prompt by typing the number of the page or pages you want to print. Separate individual pages with a comma, and use a hyphen to specify a range of pages. Use these samples as a guide:

If You Type	WordPerfect Will Print
5	Page 5 only.
1,3,5-10	Pages 1, 3, and 5 through 10.
-4	From the beginning through page 4.
6-	From page 6 to the end of the document.

Controlling the Print Quality

Two features of the Print menu allow you to control the quality of your printed output. The Text Quality option controls the quality of ordinary text output (like the documents you have already printed). The Graphics Quality option controls the quality of graphics output, such as the fonts and figures you will work with in Steps 17 and 18. Both options give you four choices for output quality: *Draft, Medium, High,* and *Do Not Print.* Select Draft or Medium quality to speed up the printing of rough drafts of your documents. Select *Do Not Print* when you want to see either text or graphic output alone for a particular document.

The default setting for text output is High and for graphic output is Medium. New print quality settings are saved with your document. Print quality settings return to the default when you clear the document from the screen.

Adding Text Enhancements

This Step covers techniques for enhancing the appearance of your documents. You will learn how to boldface, underline, center lines of text, and control line spacing. A tutorial exercise at the end of this step incorporates all of these text enhancements. (The document you create in this exercise will also be used for exercises in Steps 7 and 10.)

The techniques described here for boldface, underlining, and centering must all be used before you type your text. However, it is also possible to alter the appearance of existing text; you will learn how to add enhancements to existing sections of text in Step 10.

BOLDFACING

To boldface characters, press F6 to turn boldface on. Subsequent text will be bold until you turn boldface off by repeating the F6 command. Bold text appears brighter on screen than ordinary text.

Using F6 for boldface

Pressing the F6 key places hidden codes in your document that mark the beginning and end of a section of bold text. (You will learn more about how to work with WordPerfect's hidden codes in Step 7.) If you edit a document in which you have placed these markers, any new text you add between the markers will also be bold. You can tell when the text you are about to type will be bold by looking at the *Pos* number at the far right of the status line. When boldface is on, this number is bright; when it is off, it is dimmer than the other items in the status line.

UNDERLINING

*Using
F8 for
underlining*

Underlining is similar to boldfacing. Use the F8 key to turn underlining on and off. Underlined text is displayed in reverse video on color monitors, and is underlined on monochrome monitors. As with the Bold command, pressing F8 places codes that mark the beginning and end of the section of underlined text, and you can use the appearance of the *Pos* indicator to determine whether the text you are about to type will be underlined.

You can print text that is both underlined and boldfaced by using both F6 and F8. The order in which you press the keys is not important. To turn off either attribute, repeat the appropriate command; or press both keys again (in either order) to turn off both attributes.

CENTERING

WordPerfect provides three ways of centering text. In this step, you will learn how to center individual lines of text when you first type them. In Step 8, you will learn how to create multiple lines of centered text without having to repeat the centering command for each line. In Step 10, you will learn how to center existing, uncentered text.

STEP

6

Using
Shift-F6 for
centering

To center each line as you type, begin by using the Center command (Shift-F6) *before* you type anything on the line. This moves the cursor to the center of the screen. Once this is done, WordPerfect will adjust the text you type to keep it centered on the line. When you press Enter at the end of the line or when you fill up the line, the cursor returns to the left margin of the next line. Repeat the Center command if you want to center the text on this line as well. As with the Bold and Underline commands, the Center command places hidden codes in your document. As long as your cursor is within the bounds of these codes, you can edit centered text and the new text will be adjusted so that the line remains centered.

CONTROLLING LINE SPACING

By default, WordPerfect documents use single spacing. To set a new line spacing, use the Format: Line menu shown in Figure 6.1. To display this menu using keyboard controls, press Shift-F8, then press **1** or **L** to select Line from the resulting Format menu. To

```
Format: Line

    1 - Hyphenation              No

    2 - Hyphenation Zone - Left  10%
                          Right  4%

    3 - Justification            Left

    4 - Line Height              Auto

    5 - Line Numbering           No

    6 - Line Spacing             1

    7 - Margins - Left           1"
                  Right          1"

    8 - Tab Set                  Rel: -1", every 0.5"

    9 - Widow/Orphan Protection  No


Selection: 0
```

■ *Figure 6.1: The Format: Line menu*

Adding Text Enhancements **43**

display the same menu using pull-down menus, open the Layout menu, then select Line.

To change the line spacing, press 6 or S (or use a mouse) to select Line Spacing. This moves the cursor to the number that indicates the current line spacing. Type a new value for this item and then press Enter to change the line spacing. You needn't stick to whole numbers. For example, you can enter 1.5 if you want lines that are halfway between single and double spacing.

Cursor position and line spacing

You can change line spacing either before or after you type a section of text. When you change the spacing before you type a section of text, only subsequent text is affected; text that you have already typed is not affected. When you change the line spacing in existing text, the new spacing will take effect at the current cursor position; text above the cursor will retain the original spacing.

EXERCISE: TEXT ENHANCEMENTS

The document shown in Figure 6.2 will give you a chance to practice working with text enhancements. The instructions that follow describe how to create the document. Detailed keystrokes are given in order to ensure that your document can be used in two future exercises in this book.

1. Begin with a clear document screen.

2. To center the first line, press Shift-F6. The cursor will move to the center of the document screen. Type

    SAFETY TIPS

    then press Enter twice to end this line and create a blank line.

SAFETY TIPS

Birth to Six Months

Did you know that accidents pose one of the greatest dangers to your baby? That every year nearly **500 children under 4 years old** _die_ in California because of accidents? Most of these accidents **can be prevented.** Here are some things you can do to help ensure your child's safety.

<u>AUTO SAFETY</u>

Car crashes threaten your child's life and health. Most car injuries can be prevented by the use of approved car safety seats. Make sure that your baby's seat is installed properly. Use it **EVERY** time your child rides in your car. <u>**Obey the law; use a car seat; save your child's life.**</u>

■ *Figure 6.2: The SAFETY document*

3. Press Shift-F6 again to center the next line, then press F6 to turn on boldface. Notice the change in the *Pos* indicator. Type

   `Birth to Six Months`

4. Press F6 again to return to normal type and press Enter twice before starting the first paragraph.

5. Press Tab to make the indentation that begins the first paragraph, then copy the paragraph as it appears in Figure 6.2, using F6 to begin and end the boldface sections. Press Enter twice at the end of the paragraph.

6. Press F8 to turn on underlining (notice the change in the *Pos* indicator) and type

   `AUTO SAFETY`

   then press F8 again to turn underlining off.

STEP

6

7. Press Enter once to move to the next line. (Do not skip a line here. You will change the line spacing later in the exercise.)

8. Type the second paragraph, allowing WordPerfect to enter single-spaced lines as usual. Press F6 and F8 in sequence at the beginning and end of the section that is both bold and underlined.

9. Move the cursor to the blank line above the words <u>AUTO SAFETY.</u>

10. To open the Format: Line menu, press Shift-F8, then press **1** or **L** (or open the Layout menu, then select Line).

11. Press **6** or **S** (or use a mouse) to select Line Spacing. The cursor will move to the *1* that indicates the current line spacing.

12. Type **2** and press Enter to change to double spacing.

13. Press F7 or click the right mouse button to return to the document screen. Your line spacing should be changed so that your document now matches the one in Figure 6.2.

14. Save this document with the name SAFETY. (Press F10, type **safety**, then press Enter.) You will use it again in Steps 7 and 10.

Revealing
Formatting Codes

Each time you use a formatting command, such as for boldface or
underlining, WordPerfect inserts hidden formatting codes into
your document. In this Step, you will learn to use the WordPerfect
Reveal Codes command to view and edit these hidden codes.
Understanding how to work with formatting codes allows you to
edit your WordPerfect documents much more efficiently. An exercise following the descriptive section of this step uses the
SAFETY document created in Step 6 to demonstrate how to edit
with formatting codes.

THE REVEAL CODES DISPLAY

WordPerfect's Reveal Codes feature divides the screen into two
sections. The top section continues to display your document as
usual, while the bottom section displays a combination of text and
formatting codes. A sample Reveal Codes display is shown in
Figure 7.1. To invoke this display, press Alt-F3 (or F11 on some
12-function keyboards). If you are using pull-down menus, open

*Using
Alt-F3 to
view WP's
hidden
codes*

the Edit menu and select Reveal Codes. To return the screen to normal, *repeat the Reveal Codes command.*

Notice that you do not exit from the Reveal Codes display using any of the keystrokes that you use to exit from a WordPerfect menu (F1, F7, Spacebar, or Enter). Because the document screen is still present, these keystrokes continue to act as they normally do (when the undivided document screen is present), not as they do when a WordPerfect menu is displayed.

UNDERSTANDING WORDPERFECT'S HIDDEN CODES

Figure 7.1 shows the codes inserted in the SAFETY document created in Step 6. In the lower portion of the screen, the text of this document is interspersed with codes that are set apart from the text by the use of square brackets ([and]). Table 7.1 summarizes the formatting codes used in this document.

```
                        SAFETY TIPS

                    Birth to Six Months

        Did you know that accidents pose one of the greatest dangers
to your baby?  That every year nearly 500 children under 4 years
old die in California because of accidents?  Most of these
accidents can be prevented.  Here are some things you can do to
help ensure your child's safety.


C:\PRACTICE\SAFETY.NEW                          Doc 1 Pg 1 Ln 1.33" Pos 3.3"
[Center]SAFETY TIPS[HRt]
[HRt]
[Center][BOLD]Birth to Six Months[bold][HRt]
[HRt]
[Tab]Did you know that accidents pose one of the greatest dangers[SRt]
to your baby?  That every year nearly [BOLD]500 children under 4 years[SRt]
old[bold] [UND]die[und] in California because of accidents?  Most of these[SRt]
accidents [BOLD]can be prevented.[bold]  Here are some things you can do to[SRt]

help ensure your child's safety [HRt]

Press Reveal Codes to restore screen
```

■ *Figure 7.1: A sample Reveal Codes display*

Code	Meaning
[BOLD]	Begin boldface type
[bold]	End boldface type
[Center]	Begin centered text
[HRt]	Hard return
[Ln Spacing:*n*]	Set line spacing to value *n*
[SRt]	Soft return
[Tab]	Tab
[UND]	Begin underlining
[und]	End underlining

Table 7.1: Some Frequently Encountered Formatting Codes

Examining the SAFETY document will give you a good sense of how hidden codes are used in a WordPerfect document. The text of the first line is not centered in the Reveal Codes display; instead the **[Center]** code marks the point where you entered the Center command into the document. At the end of the line, a **[HRt]** code marks the point where you placed a hard return in the document by pressing Enter. The second line of the Reveal Codes display corresponds to a blank line that was created by pressing Enter. It contains only the **[HRt]** code. The third line of the Reveal Codes display begins with another **[Center]** code. This is followed by a **[BOLD]** code that marks the beginning of a stretch of boldface type. The end of tboldface type is marked with a lowercase **[bold]** code and the end of the line is marked with a hard return. The first line of text in the paragraph begins with a **[Tab]** code and ends with a **[SRt]** code that marks the soft return at the end of this line of text. The second line of the paragraph contains one **[BOLD]** code and ends in a soft return. The third line of the

Explanation of the codes in Figure 7.1

paragraph contains both boldface and underline codes, and also ends with a soft return code.

The last line of the paragraph ends with a hard return code.

EDITING WITH THE REVEAL CODES DISPLAY VISIBLE

WordPerfect allows you to move the cursor, enter text, and make editing changes while the Reveal Codes display is visible. Editing in this mode may seem cumbersome at first, but in the long run, it can help you avoid frustration and work more efficiently.

Moving the cursor

When you work with the Reveal Codes display, two editing cursors are visible on the screen. The document on the top of the screen uses the standard, small flashing cursor. On the bottom of the screen, the cursor is a rectangular highlight. As you use the cursor control commands, both cursors respond simultaneously, moving to equivalent locations in the two different versions of your document. When the cursor moves to a point in the document that contains a formatting code, that code is highlighted in the Reveal Codes display. Because there are no codes in the corresponding document screen, the cursor in this screen marks the character that immediately follows the highlighted code. (In Figure 7.1, the cursor is highlighting the [**BOLD**] code that precedes the word *Birth.*)

Deleting codes using Reveal Codes

You can undo any formatting command by deleting the corresponding hidden code. This is easiest to do when the Reveal Codes display is visible. Simply highlight the code you want to remove and press Del (or place the cursor immediately to the right of the code and press Backspace).

It is also possible to delete codes by pressing Del and Backspace when the Reveal Codes display is not visible. However, because it is impossible to tell whether the cursor is located on some codes (like the **[BOLD]** code) when the codes display is not visible, deleting these hidden codes requires an extra step. When you press a key that would delete a hidden code, WordPerfect displays a prompt asking you to confirm that you want to delete that code. For example, if the cursor is located on the **[BOLD]** code at the beginning of a section of bold text, the cursor in the document screen will appear to be on the first letter of that section of text. If you press the Del key when the cursor is in this location, WordPerfect will respond by displaying the following prompt on the status line:

Deleting codes without using Reveal Codes

    Delete [BOLD]? No (Yes)

The bold code will only be deleted if you respond Yes to this prompt. If you press any other key, the code remains in the document. This ensures that you won't accidentally delete codes when you mean to delete text characters. Remember, this prompt does not appear when you edit the screen in which the codes are displayed.

The location of certain codes can be satisfactorily inferred from the document screen alone. These include the **[HRt]** code that marks a hard return, and the **[Tab]** code that is inserted when you press the Tab key. When you delete these codes, no confirmation prompt appears, even when the Reveal Codes display is not visible.

Some codes, like those that mark boldface and underlining, are always present in pairs, with an uppercase code at the beginning of a section of text and a lowercase code at the end. To remove boldface or underlining from a document, you do not need to delete both codes. Deleting *either* the uppercase or the lowercase code also removes the corresponding code from your document.

Deleting paired codes

If you inadvertently delete an unpaired code, it is possible to restore it by using the Cancel command (F1), but paired codes cannot be restored in this way. To add boldface or underlining to an existing section of text, you must use the block commands covered in Step 10.

EXERCISE: EDITING WITH HIDDEN CODES

This exercise uses the SAFETY document created in Step 6 (displayed in Figure 6.2) to demonstrate editing techniques that use WordPerfect's hidden codes. The directions that follow will edit this document to match the updated version shown in Figure 7.2.

1. Retrieve the SAFETY document.

2. Press Alt-F3 (or open the Edit menu and select Reveal Codes) to display the Reveal Codes screen.

```
                          SAFETY TIPS

                      Birth to Six Months

     Did you know that accidents pose one of the greatest dangers
to your baby?  That every year nearly 500 children under 4 years
old die in California because of accidents?  Most of these
accidents can be prevented.  Here are some things you can do to
help ensure your child's safety.

AUTO SAFETY
Car crashes threaten your child's life and health.  Most car
injuries can be prevented by the use of approved car safety
seats.  Make sure that your baby's seat is installed properly.
Use it EVERY time your child rides in your car.  Obey the law;
use a car seat; save your child's life.

AVOIDING BURNS
Expect your baby to move unexpectedly.  Never eat, drink or carry
anything hot near your baby.  You can't handle both!  Keep
electric cords of irons, toasters, and electric pots out of
reach.  Reduce the temperature of your hot water to between 120
and 130 degrees Fahrenheit to avoid scalding.  If your baby does
get burned, put the burned area in cold water immediately.  Then
cover the burn loosely with a bandage and call your doctor.
```

■ *Figure 7.2: The edited version of the SAFETY document*

3. Move the cursor so that the **[Ln Spacing:2]** code between the two paragraphs is highlighted.

4. Press Del to delete this code. Because the Reveal Codes display is visible, WordPerfect deletes this code without displaying a confirmation prompt.

5. Press Home, Home, ↓ to move the cursor to the end of the document. Notice that, because you deleted the line spacing code, the entire document is now single spaced.

6. With the Reveal Codes display still visible, move the cursor to the **[und]** code at the end of the last sentence in the document. (Do not delete this code yet.)

7. Repeat the Reveal Codes command (Alt-F3) to turn the Reveal Codes display off.

8. Press Del. This will bring the following prompt to the status line:

`Delete [und]? No (Yes)`

9. Press **Y** to select Yes. As a result, the last line of the paragraph will still be in boldface, but will no longer be underlined.

10. Move the cursor to the far left of the first line of the paragraph that begins "Car crashes threaten ...." Turn the Reveal Codes display on and notice that the **[Tab]** code is highlighted, then turn the Reveal Codes display off again.

11. Press Del to delete the **[Tab]** code. Notice that this code is deleted without a confirmation prompt.

12. Move the cursor to the end of the document (Home, Home, ↓), then press Enter twice to be ready to type the heading for the second paragraph.

13. Turn the Reveal Codes display back on.

14. Press F8 to begin the underlining for the heading of the next paragraph. Notice that both the **[UND]** and the **[und]** code appear in the Reveal Codes display, with the lower-case code highlighted.

15. Type

    AVOIDING BURNS

    Notice that as you type, the characters are inserted *between* the two codes, and the **[und]** code remains highlighted.

16. Press F8 again to turn off the underlining. Notice that the cursor has now moved to the *right* of the **[und]** code. This indicates that subsequent text will not be underlined. (You can also turn off underlining or boldface by pressing the → key, because this key also moves the cursor to the right of the lowercase code.)

17. Press Enter to start the text of the new paragraph. Leave the Reveal Codes display visible while you type the paragraph as it appears in Figure 7.2.

18. Save the updated version of your document (F10, Enter, Y). You will use it again in Step 10.

As you learn new formatting commands in this book, new codes will be introduced. Take time to learn and understand these codes. This will greatly facilitate the work you do with WordPerfect.

Working with Margins

In this Step you will learn how to adjust margin size, and how to choose from among four justification styles.

SETTING MARGIN SIZE

You can set margins before you type text, or add margin settings to existing text. When you change a margin setting, WordPerfect places a hidden code in your document at the current cursor location. The setting you choose becomes effective at that point in your document. This means that if you want margin settings to be in effect throughout your document, the cursor should be at the beginning of the document when you set your margins.

Positioning the cursor for margin settings

By default, WordPerfect margins are measured in inches, and all four page margins are set to one inch from the paper's edge. (If you prefer, you can change from inches to other units of measurement using the Set-up menu, covered in Step 17.)

Left and right margins

To change left and right margins, use the Format: Line menu. To display this menu using function keys, press Shift-F8 to open the Format menu, then press **1** or **L** to select Line. (If you are using pull-down menus, open the Layout menu, then select Line.) Press **M** or **7** to select Margins from this menu. The cursor will move to where the current left margin setting is indicated. Type in a new value for the left margin, then press Enter. (You do not need to include the inch symbol.) Use decimals (for example, 1.25) to indicate fractions of an inch. The smallest allowable margin size is determined by the printer you are working with. If you select too small a margin, WordPerfect will automatically replace it with your printer's smallest setting.

After you enter a left margin setting, the cursor will then move to allow you to change the right margin setting. When you press Enter after changing this setting, the cursor will return to the *Selection* prompt at the bottom of the page. At this point, press the Spacebar or Enter if you want to return to the Format menu. Press F7 or click the right mouse button to return directly to the document screen.

When you change the left and/or right margins, WordPerfect places a margin code at the current cursor position. A sample code is shown here:

`[L/R Mar:2",2"]`

In this example, both the left and right margins have been set to two inches.

Any change you make to the left or right margins takes effect immediately. If the cursor is in the middle of a line of text when you insert a **[L/R Mar:*n*",*n*"]** code, WordPerfect will automatically move the cursor to a new line of text.

Top and bottom margins are set using the Format: Page menu. To display this menu using function keys, press Shift-F8 to open the Format menu, then press **2** or **P** to select Page. (If you are using pull-down menus, open the Layout menu, then select Page.) Use the Margins option (item 5 in this menu) to set the top and bottom margins. A margin code such as

Setting top and bottom margins

```
[T/B Mar: 1.5",1.5"]
```

will be inserted at the current cursor position. If this code is placed at the beginning of a page before any text, the new margin setting becomes effective on the current page. If the code is placed in the middle of a page, the new margin setting takes effect on the next page.

New margin settings remain in effect until a new margin code is inserted. If you want to change existing margin settings, you can insert a new margin code after the existing code. WordPerfect always uses the most recent code to format subsequent text in the current document. You can also delete margin codes after highlighting them in the Reveal Codes display. When you delete a margin code, WordPerfect uses the most recent margin setting, or reverts to the default margin setting if no other margin codes are present. Margin settings are saved as part of the document. These settings return to the default when you clear the document screen. (See Step 17 to learn how to change the initial default margin settings.)

Changing existing margin settings

If you place margin codes at the beginning of a document, and later press Home, Home, ↑ to move to the beginning of the text, WordPerfect moves the cursor to a point *after* the margin codes, but before any text. This means that you don't need to worry about accidentally entering text with the wrong margin format. If you want to move the cursor to a point at the beginning of the document *before all codes,* press Home, Home, Home, ↑.

SELECTING A JUSTIFICATION STYLE

WordPerfect 5.1 allows you to choose from four margin justification styles: *Left, Center, Right,* and *Full.* These four styles are illustrated in Figure 8.1. Full justification is the default justification style.

To select a justification style, open the Format: Line menu as described above for setting left and right margins. Press **J** or **3** to select Justification. WordPerfect will respond by displaying the following menu on the status line:

    1 Left; 2 Center; 3 Right; 4 Full

> Left justification aligns text on the left
> margin only. This style is equivalent to
> choosing No when selecting a justification
> style in WordPerfect 5.0.
>
>   Center justification
>   allows you to type several lines
>   of centered text.
>   Every line of text will be centered
>   until you enter a new justification code.
>   To accomplish the same effect
>   in WordPerfect 5.0,
>   you must center each line separately,
>   or mark a typed passage as a block and center
>   it after you have typed it.
>
>   Right justification
>   aligns text on the right margin, but not at
>   the left margin. To accomplish the same
>   effect in WordPerfect 5.0, you must use the
>   Flush Right command either as you type
>   individual lines, or on a marked block of
>   text.
>
> Full justification aligns text at both the
> right and left margins. This is the default
> style, and is equivalent to choosing Yes when
> selecting a justification style in WordPerfect
> 5.0.

■ *Figure 8.1: WordPerfect 5.1's four justification styles*

Select the justification style you want from this menu. This will insert a code such as this in your document:

`[Just:Left]`

The new justification style will take effect immediately and remain in effect until you insert a new justification code.

In the WordPerfect document screen, text is never displayed as fully justified. This means that the document screen looks identical whether you select Left or Full for a justification style. (Centered and Right justification do show up on the document screen.) If you want to check which justification style is in effect, you can use the View Document feature of the Print menu.

Creating Indented Paragraphs

You can use WordPerfect's Indent commands to create indented paragraphs. Use the Left Indent command (F4) when you want the left margin of a paragraph to be indented. Use the Left and Right Indent command (Shift-F4) when you want both the left margin and the right margin to be indented.

When you press F4 (or open the Layout menu, select Align and select Indent ->), WordPerfect moves the cursor to the next tab stop and places an [->Indent] code in the document. Any text you type after this code will be aligned to that tab stop until you press Enter. When you press Enter, the cursor will return to the original left margin. You can press F4 repeatedly to set the temporary left margin to subsequent tab stops. (See below for information about changing the default tab stops.)

When you press Shift-F4 (or open the Layout menu, select Align, and select Indent -><-), WordPerfect places an [->Indent<-] code in the document, and subsequent text is indented at both margins to the tab stops closest to each margin. When you press Enter, the margins return to their previous setting. Pressing Shift-F4 repeatedly narrows the width of the text by one tab stop on either side of the page for each time you press the command.

You also can add indentation commands to existing text. When you do this, the text is indented until the next [HRt] code.

Working with Tabs

In this Step, you learn how to position tab settings and how to work with WordPerfect's four tab styles. The exercise at the end of the Step demonstrates tab-setting techniques. (You will use the document you create in this exercise again in Step 11.)

DISPLAYING THE TAB RULER LINE

WordPerfect's default tab setting places tabs at half-inch intervals. To change this setting, use the Format: Line menu. To display this menu, press Shift-F8, then press **1** or **L** (or open the Layout menu, then select Line). Press **8** or **T** (or use the mouse) to select Tab Set. WordPerfect will respond by displaying a ruler line like the one shown in Figure 9.1 In this figure, tab settings are marked with the letter L. Other letters are used to mark a variety of tab styles, as explained below. You use the tab ruler line to select tab styles, to delete existing tabs, and to insert new tabs.

SELECTING A TAB TYPE

Absolute vs. relative tabs

WordPerfect 5.1 tabs can be set at a given distance from the edge of the printed page, or relative to the current left margin setting. Tabs set with respect to the printed page are known as *absolute* tabs. Those set relative to the current margin are known as *relative* tabs. When you are working with relative tabs, the current left margin is always given as 0 on the ruler line, and tab positions are marked with a + or a −, depending on whether they are to the right or the left of the margin. Relative tabs are the default choice and the ruler line in Figure 9.1 uses this tab style. When you are working with absolute tabs, the left edge of the paper is 0 regardless of where the left margin has been set, and tab settings are not preceded by either a plus or a minus sign. (Earlier versions of WordPerfect used only this tab style.) If you set tabs using the relative tab type, you can change the left margin position and the tabs will automatically change to remain in the same position with respect to the new margin. Absolute tabs retain their

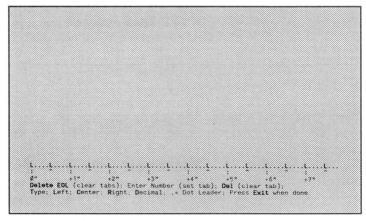

■ *Figure 9.1: The ruler line for setting tabs*

position with respect to the left edge of the page, regardless of the left margin setting.

To select a tab type, display the tab ruler line on screen and select Type from the menu at the bottom of the screen. This will bring up the following menu:

`Tab Type: 1 Absolute; 2 Relative to Margin`

Select the tab type you want from this menu. When you do, the ruler line will change to reflect the choice you made.

CLEARING EXISTING TABS

You can clear existing tabs individually, or you can clear the entire ruler line. To clear individual tabs, use the ← or → key to move to the letter that marks the tab you want to delete, then press Del.

To clear all the tabs to the right of the current cursor position, press Ctrl-End. This is the Delete to End of Line command. This is what is referred to where you see *Delete EOL* in the instructions on the ruler line screen. To delete all current tabs, press Home, Home, ← to move the cursor to the left edge of the page, then press Ctrl-End to delete all existing tabs. (If you are working with relative tabs and press Home-← from any position to the right of the 0, the cursor will move to the left margin, rather than the left edge of the paper, and you can delete the tabs from that point.)

SETTING NEW TABS

WordPerfect 5.1 allows you to set tabs in any one of four styles: *Left, Center, Right,* and *Decimal.* Left tabs align material at the left edge; center tabs center material around the tab stop; right tabs align material at the right edge; and decimal tabs align material on the decimal or on any character you select for this purpose. These four styles are illustrated in Figure 9.2.

To select a tab style, type the letter that corresponds to that style when you place a tab setting on the ruler line. Use **L** for Left tabs, **C** for Center tabs, **R** for Right tabs, and **D** for Decimal tabs. (Use either uppercase or lowercase letters to select a tab style.)

WordPerfect allows you to set individual tabs in either of the following two ways:

Setting individual tabs

- Use ← and → to move the cursor to the position you want, then press a letter (**L**, **C**, **R**, or **D**) to select a tab style and place a tab in that position. (You can use any combination of the four tab styles.)

- Type any number and press Enter to place a left tab at that point on the ruler line, regardless of the current cursor position. (For example, press **3** Enter to enter a tab at 3".) If you wish, type **C**, **R**, or **D** to change to another tab style after the tab location has been entered, but before you move the cursor from that location.

If you want to set tabs at a position whose inch value is between zero and one, type the number 0 before you type the decimal that corresponds to the tab position you desire. For example, to set a tab at a position one-half inch from the margin, you would have to enter 0.5. This is necessary because pressing the period before you

LEFT	CENTER	RIGHT	DECIMAL
January	January	January	January
May	May	May	May
December	December	December	December
123	123	123	123
45.75	45.75	45.75	45.75
12,986.5	12,986.5	12,986.5	12,986.5

■ *Figure 9.2: WordPerfect's four tab styles*

type anything serves a special function; it places dot leaders in front of any text you place using a tab setting. (You might use this feature if you were typing a table of contents or a cast list and wanted dots to separate two columns of items.)

You may also want to set tabs at uniform intervals. To do this, have the ruler line on screen, clear the existing tabs, then proceed as follows:

- Type a number that corresponds to where you want the tab settings to start, then type a comma (,), followed by the size of the interval you want to separate the tabs.

Setting tabs at intervals

For example, to set tabs at one-inch intervals starting at the left margin, you would type

```
0,1
```

then press Enter.

After you have set tabs where you want them, press F7 or click the right mouse button to return to the Format: Line menu. Repeat this to return to the document screen.

Returning to your document

Each time you set tabs, WordPerfect places a tab-set code in your document that identifies the type of tab (Rel or Abs) and the tab positions you chose. (Tab-set codes do not distinguish between the four tab styles.) To change tab settings, either move the cursor to a position after the last tab-set code and repeat the tab-setting process, or delete the tab-set code if you want to return to a previous tab setting. Like margin codes, tab-set codes are saved with the document and return to the default setting when you clear the document screen.

EXERCISE: SETTING TABS

The exercise that follows demonstrates tab-setting techniques. When you are done, save the short document you have created. You will use it again in Step 11 to search for the tab-set code. Begin with a clear document screen.

1. Press Tab. The *Pos* indicator should show that the cursor is at 1.5" (the first default tab after the one-inch left margin).

2. Type the following, and leave the cursor at the end of the second sentence:

   ```
   When you set a WordPerfect tab, a code is
   placed at the current cursor location.
   These codes affect only subsequent text.
   ```

3. To display the tab ruler line, press Shift-F8 (or open the Layout menu), select Line, then select Tab Set.

4. Press Home, Home, ← to move the cursor to the left edge of the paper (indicated as -1"), then press Ctrl-End to delete the existing tabs.

5. Type **2**, then press Enter to set a left tab two inches from the left margin.

6. Type **4**, press Enter, then type **C** to set a Center tab four inches from the left margin.

7. Press F7 twice or click the right mouse button twice to return to the document screen.

8. Press Enter to move to a new line.

9. Press Tab. The *Pos* indicator should show that the cursor is now at 3". (This is because the 2" setting you used is *relative* to the 1" left margin.) Type

   ```
   Left Tab
   ```

10. Press Tab again. This will move the cursor to *Pos 5"*, where you set a Center tab. Watch the screen as you type the following:

```
Center Tab
```

Notice that the text remains centered around the tab stop.

11. Save the document using the name TABS. You will use this document again in Step 11.

After you have saved the document, use the Reveal Codes screen (Alt-F3) to locate the tab-set code. Try moving the cursor to positions both before and after this code. Notice the change in the highlighted bar that divides the screen as you move the cursor above and below the tab setting. This bar uses triangles to mark the current tab settings. When you are done, clear the screen without saving any changes you have made to the original document (F7, N, N).

Viewing tab settings

Working with Blocks of Text

In this Step, you will learn how to work with marked blocks of text. You can use marked blocks as a convenient way to copy, delete, or move larger sections of text. You can also mark blocks of text when you want to use a variety of WordPerfect features such as underlining, centering, and boldface within a section of text.

THE WORDPERFECT BLOCK COMMAND

The WordPerfect Block command allows you to highlight a section of text and/or formatting codes of any length. It is possible to do this using either the keyboard or a mouse. Once you have marked the text, a variety of commands is available for manipulating the marked block.

Marking Blocks of Text

To mark a block of text with the keyboard, move the cursor to the beginning of the section you want to work with, then press Alt-F4.

Using the keyboard

69

This will turn on the Block command and produce a flashing display in the lower-left corner of the screen that reads Block on. When the Block command is on, you can highlight a section of text using any combination of these two techniques:

- Use WordPerfect's cursor control commands to extend the highlighting in either direction.

- Press any keyboard character to extend the highlighting forward to that character from its current position. (For example, press the period to highlight to the end of a sentence, or press t to highlight to the next occurrence of the letter t.)

You can turn Block off and remove block highlighting by pressing F1.

Using a mouse

To mark a block of text using a mouse, position the mouse cursor at the beginning of the section of text you want to mark, then hold down the left mouse button and drag the mouse on your work surface. As you do, the text on screen will be highlighted. Release the left button when you have highlighted the section of text you want to work with.

Hold the left button down until you are sure you have selected the text you want. Once you have released the left button, pressing it again removes the highlighting and turns Block off. (This is equivalent to pressing the F1 key.)

Moving, Copying, and Deleting Marked Text

Once you have selected a section of text, you can move, copy, or delete that text with either the WordPerfect Move command (Ctrl-F4) or, if you are working with pull-down menus, with commands in the Edit menu.

If you press Ctrl-F4 *when a section of text has already been highlighted,* the following menu of options appears on the status line:

    1 Block; 2 Tabular Column; 3 Rectangle

Select Block to work with all the highlighted text. (Options 2 and 3 are useful if you want to work with columns of text.) This will bring the following Block/Move menu to the status line:

    1 Move; 2 Copy; 3 Delete; 4 Append

These options have the following effects:

■ Select *Move* to remove the highlighted text from its present location and insert it in a new location.

■ Select *Copy* to leave the highlighted text in its present location and also insert a copy of it in a new location.

■ Select *Delete* to remove the highlighted text.

■ Select *Append* to add the highlighted text to a different file.

If you are using pull-down menus, you can select any of these four options by opening the Edit menu after you have marked a block of text and selecting the option you want from that menu.

If you select Move or Copy, you will see the following prompt on the status line:

    Move cursor; Press Enter to retrieve

When you see this prompt, move the editing cursor to the location you want the moved or copied text to occupy, and press Enter. The marked block will be inserted in front of the cursor.

If you press F1 or click the right mouse button, the *Move cursor* prompt disappears. You can use this technique to cancel a Move or Copy command. After you have canceled the command, you can still retrieve the text by using the following command sequence: Ctrl-F4, Retrieve, Block. This command sequence will continue to retrieve the same block of text until you select a new block of text to move or copy.

If you select the Delete option from the Block/Move menu shown above, the marked text is deleted immediately, with no further prompts. A second, quicker alternative is also available for deleting marked blocks of text. Simply press the Delete (Del) key. When the Block command is on, this key deletes the entire marked block. You will be prompted to confirm that you want to delete the marked text with this question:

`Delete Block? No (Yes)`

Select Yes in response to this prompt to complete the process.

If you select Append from the Block/Move menu, you will be prompted to enter a file name. If you enter the name of an existing file, the text will be added to the end of that file. If you enter a new file name, WordPerfect will create a file in the current default directory with that name and place the selected text in the file.

Using Other Features with Marked Text

You can also use a variety of other WordPerfect features on marked blocks of text. One such feature is boldface. To add boldface to existing text, mark the text as a block, then press F6 to select boldface for the marked text. Table 10.1 summarizes several additional features that you can use in this way.

Feature	Keystroke	Effect When Block Is On
Bold	F6	Changes marked text to boldface.
Case Conversion	Shift-F3	Changes marked text to uppercase or lowercase.
Center	Shift-F6	Centers marked text.
Delete	Del or Backspace	Deletes marked text.
Flush Right	Alt-F6	Right-justifies marked text.
Print	Shift-F7	Prints marked text.
Save	F10	Saves marked text to a new file.
Underline	F8	Underlines marked text.

Table 10.1: Manipulating Marked Blocks of Text

SHORTCUTS FOR WORKING WITH SENTENCES, PARAGRAPHS, AND PAGES

WordPerfect provides a shortcut if you want to copy, delete, or move a section of text that is exactly one sentence, one paragraph, or one page long. (Sentences are delineated by periods, paragraphs by hard returns, and pages by either soft or hard page breaks.) When this is the case, you needn't begin by marking the section of text you want to manipulate. Begin instead by positioning the cursor anywhere in the sentence, paragraph, or page you want to

Using Ctrl-F4 with Block off

work with, then press Ctrl-F4. When the Block command is not on, this will bring the following prompt to the status line:

1 Sentence; **2** Paragraph; **3** Page; **4** Retrieve

When you select options 1, 2, or 3 from this menu, WordPerfect will automatically highlight the amount of text you selected and follow it with the same prompts you would have seen had you marked the text with the Block command manually. You can use option 4 to retrieve the most recently moved or copied text. (If you select the Retrieve option, select Block from the next menu to retrieve the text.)

This shortcut only works when you want to move, copy, or delete text. If you want to use one of the features summarized in Table 10.1, you must mark the text manually using either Alt-F4 or the mouse.

EXERCISE: WORKING WITH THE BLOCK COMMAND

For this exercise, retrieve the SAFETY document as modified in Step 7 (see Figure 7.2). You will add boldface to a marked section of text, use the shortcut to delete a paragraph, and finally use block commands to move a section of text that includes a title and a paragraph. The resulting version of the document is shown in Figure 10.1.

1. Move the cursor to the first letter of the centered title "SAFETY TIPS."

2. Press Alt-F4 to turn the Block command on, then press End to move the cursor to the end of this line of text. The entire title should now be highlighted.

```
                    SAFETY TIPS

                  Birth to Six Months

AVOIDING BURNS
Expect your baby to move unexpectedly. Never eat, drink or carry
anything hot near your baby. You can't handle both! Keep
electric cords of irons, toasters, and electric pots out of
reach. Reduce the temperature of your hot water to between 120
and 130 degrees Fahrenheit to avoid scalding. If your baby does
get burned, put the burned area in cold water immediately. Then
cover the burn loosely with a bandage and call your doctor.


AUTO SAFETY
Car crashes threaten your child's life and health. Most car
injuries can be prevented by the use of approved car safety
seats. Make sure that your baby's seat is installed properly.
Use it EVERY time your child rides in your car. Obey the law;
use a car seat; save your child's life.
```

■ *Figure 10.1: The final version of the SAFETY document*

3. Press F6 to convert the highlighted text to boldface.

4. Move the cursor to any position in the introductory paragraph.

5. To delete the paragraph, press Ctrl-F4, select Paragraph from the first menu, and then select Delete from the second menu.

6. Press Home, Home, ↓, then Enter to ensure that there is a blank line at the end of the document.

7. Move the cursor to the blank line above the heading AUTO SAFETY.

8. To mark this heading and the attached paragraph, press Alt-F4, then press ↓ until the entire paragraph is highlighted. The cursor should now be on the blank line between paragraphs.

9. To move the marked text, press Ctrl-F4, select Block from the first menu, then select Move from the second menu. The paragraph will disappear and you will see this message

on the status line:

```
Move cursor; Press Enter to retrieve
```

10. Move the cursor to the blank line at the end of the document and press Enter to move the AUTO SAFETY paragraph to the end of the document.

Your document should now match Figure 10.1. (This is the final version of the SAFETY document, so you do not need to save the updated version.)

11

Using Search
and Replace

Many editing tasks can be made easier by using WordPerfect's Search and Replace features. The Search command allows you to search either forward or backward for specific elements in your document. Using the Replace command, you can systematically replace existing sections of text with new text.

THE SEARCH COMMAND

WordPerfect's Search command can be used to search for text characters and formatting codes, or a combination of both. Searching for text characters is a quick way to locate specific portions of a document. Searching for formatting codes allows you to delete or replace these codes quickly and easily, without having to search the Reveal Codes screen to find them.

All WordPerfect searches are conducted starting at the current cursor location. To search forward from the cursor, either press F2 or *Forward search* open the Search menu and select Forward. This brings the following prompt to the status line.

    `-> Srch:`

Use this prompt to specify the text or codes you want to find. This is your *search string*. (For more information about search strings, see "Searching for Text" and "Searching for Codes," below.) Once you have typed the search string, initiate the search in one of the following ways:

- Press F2 again.

- Press Esc.

- Double-click the left mouse button. (A double click is two clicks in close succession.)

WordPerfect will respond by moving the cursor to a position immediately *following* the next occurrence of the search string. (Notice that pressing Enter is *not* a method of initiating a search.) If no match is found, the message

    `* Not found *`

will be displayed on the status line.

Repeating a search

To repeat a forward search for the same string, you can either press F2 twice, or open the Search menu and select Next. Until you enter a new search string, WordPerfect automatically displays the previous string when you initiate a new Search command. (This is true even if you have changed to a new document.) If you don't want to repeat a search for the previous string, you can type a new search string without deleting the existing one. As soon as you type a character, the existing string disappears.

Backward search

To search backward from the cursor, either press Shift-F2 or open the Search menu and select Backward. The resulting status line prompt, shown below, begins with a left-pointing arrow rather than a right-pointing arrow.

```
<- Srch:
```

Enter your text and/or codes in response to this prompt, then initiate the search as you would for a forward search.

You can change the direction of a search when either the forward or backward search prompt is displayed by pressing either ↑ (to switch to backward search) or ↓ (to switch to forward search).

Searching for Text

When you type a search string consisting of text, you can type individual words or whole phrases. When you type a phrase, WordPerfect matches it character for character, including spaces you enter between words, as well as the words themselves.

When you enter a single word as a search string, WordPerfect will locate that word where it occurs independently, and also where it occurs as part of a longer word. For example, if you wanted to search for the word *and,* WordPerfect would stop the search at s*and* and at *And*erson as well as at *and.*

Word searches

You can take advantage of this to simplify searches. For example, you might type just *fig* in order to find instances of the word *figure.* If you want to limit the search to those places where the search string is an entire word, you can type a space before and/or after the word. However, be careful with this technique. A word at the beginning of a paragraph is often preceded by a tab code or hard return code rather than a space. Similarly, a word at the end of a sentence is followed by a period rather than a space. Don't include spaces in your search string if you think the word you are looking for might be located in such a place.

**Capital-
ization**

If you type your search string in lowercase letters, WordPerfect ignores case when it performs the search. If, for example, you enter a search string as *california,* the search would stop at *California* and *CALIFORNIA* as well. If you include uppercase letters in your search string, the search will only stop when the case as well as the letters match. For example, if the search string is entered as *Joseph,* the search would stop at *Joseph* or *JOSEPH* (which both begin with an uppercase J), but not at *joseph* (which begins with a lowercase j). If you enter the search string as *JOSEPH,* the search will only stop at *JOSEPH.*

**Wildcard
characters**

You may want to search for a string in which one or more characters vary. For example, you might want to find every instance of a letter in square brackets ([A], [B], [C], and so on). For this example, you need the second character to be a wildcard. You can introduce a wildcard character into a search string by using the Ctrl-X (^X) symbol. To introduce this symbol into a search string, begin by pressing Ctrl-V wherever you want the wildcard character. When you do this, the search prompt is replaced by a prompt that reads

```
Key =
```

Press Ctrl-X in response to this prompt. Your search string will reappear with the ^X symbol inserted at the current cursor location. To conduct a forward search for the bracketed letters in the example, the keystroke sequence would be: F2, [, Ctrl-V, Ctrl-X,], F2.

Searching for Codes

WordPerfect also allows you to search for formatting codes in your document. To search for a code, initiate the search command as usual. Then, at the search prompt, repeat the keystrokes you used when you entered that code into your document. When you do this, the formatting code is entered on the status line after the search prompt. For example, to search for places where you used boldface, you would press F6 at the search prompt. The resulting status line display would be

```
-> Srch: [BOLD]
```

You can then continue as you would for any other search (by pressing F2).

You can include more than one code or a mixture of codes and text in any search string. For instance, to find a location where you typed the word *section* at the beginning of a line (after pressing the Enter key), you could press Enter and then type *section* in response to the search prompt. The resulting status line display would look like this:

Combining codes and text

```
-> Srch: [HRt]section
```

In the exercise that follows, you will locate the tab set code you placed in the TABS document that was created at the end of Step 9.

1. Retrieve the TABS document and place the cursor at the beginning of the document.

2. Press F2 (or open the Search menu and select Forward) to initiate a forward search.

3. Press Shift-F8 (the first keystroke in the function key sequence you use to set tabs). The status line will change to read

```
1 Line; 2 Page; 3 Other: 0
```

4. Press 1 or L to select Line. This will display a menu of eight choices. Press 7 or T to select Tab Set from this

menu. The status line should now read:

`-> Srch: [Tab Set]`

5. Press F2 or Esc to initiate the search. The cursor should stop at the end of the second line of text—the position where your cursor was when you set the tabs.

6. Press Alt-F3 to display the hidden codes and verify that the cursor is now located just after the tab-set code.

A search like this one is useful when you want to delete an existing code, or insert a new code to update the existing one. If you reset the tabs without changing the cursor position after a search, the new code will immediately follow the original code. As a result, the original tab setting will be overridden by the newly inserted one.

THE REPLACE COMMAND

Use the Replace command when you want to systematically replace a repeated item in a document. Sample applications for the Replace command include correcting a frequently occurring misspelling or updating a document by replacing a person's name with a new one.

To initiate a Replace command, either press Alt-F2 or open the Search menu and select Replace. As a result, you will see this prompt on the status line:

`w/ Confirm? No (Yes)`

Performing a global replace

If you respond No to this prompt, WordPerfect will replace the search string throughout the searched portion of your document without consulting you for confirmation at each occurrence of the string.

Although No is the default response, using this response is risky. You might find that it produces results that you did not anticipate, and these errors are difficult to find and fix. For example, you might want to update a document by replacing the word *black* with the term *African-American.* If you performed this operation without confirmation in a document containing the word *blackboard,* this word would be transformed into *African-Americanboard.* As a general rule, always save a backup copy of your document before you perform an unconfirmed replace.

If you select Yes in response to the confirmation prompt, Word-Perfect will stop at each instance where the search string is found, and prompt you to confirm whether you want the replacement to take place at that location.

After you have responded to the confirmation prompt, you will see the search prompt:

`-> Srch:`

(You can press ↑ at this point if you want to perform a backward replace operation.) In response to this prompt, type the word or phrase you want to replace, then press F2, then Esc, or double-click the left mouse button. When you do this, you will see this prompt:

`Replace with:`

Enter the appropriate replacement word or phrase, then initiate the Replace operation by pressing F2, then Esc, or by double-clicking the left mouse button.

If you responded No to the confirmation prompt, the corrections will be made automatically throughout the searched portion of the document.

Performing a confirmed replace

If you responded Yes to the confirmation prompt that appeared when you first began the Replace operation, WordPerfect will stop when it finds the first search string and display this additional confirmation prompt:

`Confirm? No (Yes)`

If you respond Yes to this prompt, the replacement is made and WordPerfect searches for the next occurrence of the search string. If you respond No, the replacement is not made and the search also continues.

Capitalization in Replace operations

Rules for including capitalization in the search string of a Replace operation are the same as for a simple Search operation. WordPerfect also automatically matches capitalization if you do not include uppercase letters in your replacement string. For example, if you enter *left* as a search string, and *right* as a replacement string, WordPerfect would use *Right* (with an uppercase R) as the replacement whenever it encountered *Left* (with an uppercase L) in your document. If you include any uppercase letters in your replacement string, WordPerfect uses that case regardless of the case it finds in your document. This means that you could replace *wordperfect* with *WordPerfect,* or replace *city* with *Berkeley* by using the correct capitalization in the replacement string.

Checking Spelling

This Step covers the use of WordPerfect's online dictionary for correcting spelling. The Spell command allows you to check the spelling of individual words, pages, or an entire document. The online dictionary it uses for this purpose is extensive, containing a wide variety of technical and medical terms as well as those words you would expect to find in a standard desktop dictionary. You can also supplement the existing dictionary with a supplemental online dictionary. The supplemental dictionary can include additional words, abbreviations, and/or proper names that you use frequently. The Spell command includes additional options that allow you to look up word spellings and to count the number of words in your document.

CHECKING SPELLING

To invoke the Spell command, either press Ctrl-F2, or open the Tools menu and select Spell. This brings the Spell menu to the status line. The first three items in this menu are:

   1 **W**ord; 2 **P**age; 3 **D**ocument

(If you move the cursor, this menu will disappear.) Select *Word* to check the spelling of the word at the current cursor location, select *Page* to check the spelling of the page containing the cursor, and select *Document* to check the entire document. When you select Document, the entire document is checked, regardless of the current cursor location. (You can interrupt the spell-checking process before the entire document has been searched by pressing F1.) When WordPerfect encounters a word that is not in one of the on-line dictionaries, the program highlights the misspelled word, splits the screen, and displays a Not Found screen like the one shown in Figure 12.1.

This screen lists a variety of properly spelled words that are offered as suggestions that you might want to use to replace the misspelled word. If you find the word you intended to use on this list,

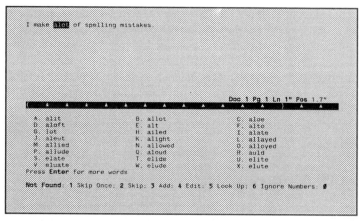

■ *Figure 12.1: A sample Not Found screen*

you can replace the misspelled word in your document by pressing the letter that precedes the correctly spelled word. When you do this, WordPerfect automatically adjusts letters to uppercase if you used uppercase letters in your document. For example, *Mispell* would be replaced by *Misspell* and *MISPELL* would be replaced by *MISSPELL*.

Use the menu at the bottom of the Spell screen when you do not find the correctly spelled word in the list of suggestions, or if WordPerfect has highlighted a proper name or an abbreviation that is correct as it stands. The items in this menu have the following functions:

Skip Once   Leaves the word as it is. Spell checking continues and will stop at subsequent occurrences of the word.

Skip   Leaves the word as it is, continues spell checking, and skips all subsequent occurrences of the word.

Add   Adds the word to the Supplementary dictionary and continues spell checking.

Edit   Moves cursor to the document so you can edit a mistake. Press F7 to complete the editing and continue spell checking.

Look Up   Look up the correct spelling. (See below.)

Ignore Numbers   Skips over subsequent situations where a "word" is not found because it involves a combination of letters and numbers (for example, 62nd or F2).

(To change the misspelling in Figure 12.1 from *alot* to *a lot,* you would have to use the Edit option.)

The Look Up option

WordPerfect is able to suggest correct spelling alternatives for some very badly misspelled words (for example, *nolej* for *knowledge)* because the spelling program uses both phonetics and letter arrangement to create the list of suggestions. But it is inevitable that some misspelled words (for example, *arciteture* for *architecture)* will result in no suggested alternatives. The Look Up feature allows you to look up words when you are unsure of the spelling and WordPerfect has not succeeded in suggesting the correct alternative. The Look Up option is included on both the original Spell menu and also on the Not Found menu that appears when a misspelled word has been located. (It is item 5 in both menus.) When you select this option, WordPerfect displays this prompt:

`Word or word pattern:`

In response to this prompt, you can enter a word pattern that consists of only portions of the word you want to look up. In place of individual letters you are unsure of, you can enter a question mark (?), or if you are unsure of a string of unknown length, you can enter an asterisk (*). For example, to look up the correct spelling of *architecture,* you might enter *ar*ure.* WordPerfect would respond by listing any words in its dictionary that begin with *ar* and end in *ure.* (In this case, the list would include *architecture* and *armature.)* If you don't succeed in finding the word with your first attempt, you can press F7 to enter a new word pattern.

Be aware that no spell checker can catch all spelling and/or typographical errors. For example, if you typed *tow* or *to* instead of *two,* the mistake could not be caught with the WordPerfect Spell command, because the misspelled versions of *two* are correctly spelled words that would be found in the online dictionary.

WORDPERFECT'S DICTIONARIES

WordPerfect looks for each word it checks in two dictionaries. The dictionary provided with the program is contained in a file called WP{WP}US.LEX. This dictionary is generally located in the C:\WP51 directory. When you use the Add option, WordPerfect adds words to a supplemental dictionary that is created automatically the first time you use this option. By default, this dictionary is also located in the C:\WP51 directory and is called WP{WP}US.SUP.

WordPerfect will automatically search the C:\WP51 directory for dictionary files. If you receive a message saying that the dictionary was not found, check the C:\WP51 directory for the dictionary files.

It is possible to edit the supplementary dictionary. To do this, you can change to the C:\WP51 directory and retrieve the WP{WP}US.SUP file as you would any ordinary document file. Words in this file are arranged alphabetically and separated by a hard return. You can edit these words, or delete them entirely. You can also add words to this file. When you are done, save the updated file as you would any other.

SPECIAL SPELL FEATURES

In addition to checking word spelling, WordPerfect's spell checker looks for other common typographical errors. These include the presence of double words and words with an irregular arrangement of uppercase and lowercase letters.

If you have typed two identical words in succession, WordPerfect highlights these words during a spell checking operation and

Double words

displays the Double Word menu. The four items in this menu are used as follows:

Skip	Skips this instance of the double word, continues spell checking, and stops at subsequent occurrences of the same word pair.
Delete 2nd	Deletes the second word of the pair and continues spell checking.
Edit	Moves cursor to the document so you can edit either or both words. Press F7 to complete the editing and continue spell checking.
Disable Double Word Checking	Ignores double words for remainder of the document.

Irregular case

If you have typed a word with an unusual arrangement of upper-case and lowercase letters, WordPerfect stops and displays the Irregular Case menu during spell checking. Examples of irregular case include two initial uppercase letters (THat), or uppercase letters following lowercase letters (tHAT). The Irregular Case menu includes Skip, Edit, and Disable options that act like those for the double word menu. This menu also includes a Replace option. When you choose Replace, WordPerfect changes the case of letters in your word to the pattern that is most likely to be correct, based on what it found in your document. For example, *THat* would be replaced by *That,* and *tHAT* would be replaced by *THAT.* (Note that this pattern may not always be what you intended.)

Using the Thesaurus

In this Step, you will learn how to use WordPerfect's online the-saurus to find word synonyms.

THE THESAURUS COMMAND

To initiate the Thesaurus command, either press Alt-F1, or open the Tools menu and select Thesaurus. WordPerfect will respond by displaying a list of synonyms of the word at the current cursor lo-cation. If the cursor is not on a word when you invoke the com-mand, WordPerfect will prompt you to enter a word by displaying the prompt

`Word:`

on the status line.

THESAURUS SCREEN

Figure 13.1 shows a sample Thesaurus screen that was created by placing the cursor on the word *test*. Notice that in this example there are both noun (n) and verb (v) meanings listed. Thesaurus listings also include adjective (a) and antonym (ant) lists when these are appropriate. (Look up *black* or *high* to see examples of adjective and antonym listings.)

Words marked with a bullet (•) on a Thesaurus screen are known as *headwords*. When you press the letter preceding a head-word, WordPerfect displays the synonyms associated with that headword.

(If you have requested additional word lists, the bold letters that precede the headwords move from column to column. If you want to look up a bulleted word that is not preceded by a bold letter,

```
This is a test of the WordPerfect thesaurus.


┌test-(n)─────────────────────────────────────────────────────┐
│ 1 A  •comprehensive        •verify                           │
│   B  •examination                                            │
│   C  •final             5  •analyze                          │
│   D  •quiz                 •inspect                           │
│   E  •review               •investigate                      │
│                            •probe                            │
│ 2 F  •essay                                                  │
│   G  •experiment        6  •examine                          │
│   H  •trial                •question                         │
│                            •quiz                             │
│ 3 I  •analysis                                               │
│   J  •inquiry                                                │
│   K  •investigation                                          │
│test-(v)──────────────                                        │
│ 4 L  •check                                                  │
│   M  •prove                                                  │
│   N  •try                                                    │
│ 1 Replace Word; 2 View Doc; 3 Look Up Word; 4 Clear Column: 0│
└─────────────────────────────────────────────────────────────┘
```

■ *Figure 13.1: A sample Thesaurus screen*

you can press ← or → to move the bold letters to the appropriate column of words.)

The items in the Thesaurus menu have the following effects:

Replace Word   Allows you to replace the word in your document with any word in the list on screen by pressing the letter preceding that word.

View Doc   Moves the cursor to your document and allows you to scroll through the text. Press F7 to return to the Thesaurus.

Look Up Word   Displays the *Word:* prompt that allows you to look up another word.

Clear Column   Clears the screen of the most recent list of words.

Use F7, F1, or the right mouse button to exit from the Thesaurus.

Multiple-Page Documents

This Step covers techniques you can use to manage multiple-page documents. These techniques include controlling page breaks, positioning page numbers, and creating headers and/or footers.

CONTROLLING PAGE BREAKS

Normally, WordPerfect automatically starts a new page when the text you are typing has filled the current page. Wherever this occurs, a single dashed line appears on screen, and a soft page code ([**SPg**]) is inserted in your document. If you want to start a new page at any other point in a document, you can do so by pressing Ctrl-Enter. This is the Hard Page command, which places a hard page code ([**HPg**]) at the current cursor position. Hard page breaks are indicated by a double dashed line on screen.

Hard page breaks

The Hard Page command is easy to use, but you should be aware that this command means that a new page will always start at the marked position, regardless of any editing changes you make.

This is appropriate in some instances, for example, at the end of a chapter. It is not the best way to control page breaks in other situations, such as when you want to keep a paragraph from being split onto two pages, because the paragraph might be moved to the middle of a page by later editing changes. For situations such as this, you can use a Block Protect command.

Block Protect

The Block Protect feature allows you to mark blocks of text that should be kept together on one page. If a marked block is too long to fit on the current page, it is moved as a unit onto the next page. To use the Block Protect Feature, highlight the text you want to protect using the Block command (see Step 10), then press Shift-F8 (or open the Edit menu and select Protect Block). When Block is on, this command displays the following prompt on screen:

```
Protect Block? No (Yes)
```

Press **Y** to confirm that you want to protect the marked block of text. This places a pair of codes ([**Block Pro:On**] and [**Block Pro:Off**]) at either end of the selected text. Any text located between these codes will be kept together on a page. You can add material to a protected block without affecting block protection, as long as the material you add remains between these two codes. Deleting either code removes the other, and cancels block protection.

POSITIONING PAGE NUMBERS

By default, WordPerfect does not automatically number the pages in longer documents. You can include page numbers and control their position on the page with the Format: Page Number Position menu shown in Figure 14.1. (An alternate way to add page numbers to a document is by including them within headers or footers, as described below.)

To open the Page Number Position menu, press Shift-F8 (or open the Layout menu), select Page, select Page Numbering, then select Page Number Position. This menu includes a map of eight possible page number placement styles. To select one of these styles, press the number that corresponds to the placement position you want. Press F7 (or click the right mouse button) to return to the document screen.

This places a page numbering code such as this one at the current cursor position:

[Pg numbering: Top Left]

If the page numbering code is at the beginning of a page, page numbering will begin on that page, using the current page number as it appears on the status line. If there is text on the page above the code, page numbering will begin with the next page.

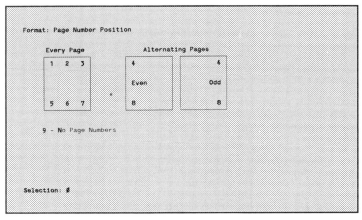

■ *Figure 14.1: The Format: Page Number Position menu*

You can suppress page numbering on a single page with the Format: Suppress menu, or on all subsequent pages by using the Page
Number Position menu to turn page numbering off.

To suppress page numbering on the current page, move the cursor
to the top of the page, press Shift-F8 (or open the Layout menu),
select Page, select Suppress (this page only), then select Suppress
Page Numbering. This will move the cursor to the Suppress Page
Numbering option. Press **Y** to change this option to Yes, then
press F7 to return to the document screen. A **[Suppress: PgNum]**
code will be inserted at the current cursor position. Page numbering will be suppressed on the current page, and will continue automatically on the next page, using the correct numbering. If, for
example, you suppress page numbering at the top of the first page
of a document, numbering will start on the second page using the
numeral 2. (You can also use the Format: Suppress menu to suppress headers and footers, which are introduced later in this Step.)

To turn page numbering off on all subsequent pages, move the cursor to the top of the first page that you want to be unnumbered,
open the Format: Page Number Position menu (Shift-F8, P,N,P), then
select No Page Numbers. Press F7 to return to your document.

HEADERS AND FOOTERS

Use headers and footers to display repetitive material on every
page of a document without having to retype the material on each
individual page. Items commonly included in headers and footers
include dates, chapter titles, section names, and page numbers.
(This book uses left-justified footers on even pages for the page
number and book title, and right-justified footers on odd pages for
the Step title and page number.)

Creating Headers and Footers

You can add headers or footers at any point in a document. When you do, a code is placed in your document at the current cursor position, and the header or footer you created is used on all subsequent pages. To begin a header or footer on the current page, the cursor must be positioned at the top of that page.

To define a new header or footer, open the Format: Page menu by pressing Shift-F8 (or opening the Layout menu), then selecting Page. Select either Header (item 3) or Footer (item 4) from this menu. Depending on your choice, one of the two menus shown here will appear at the bottom of your screen:

1 Header **A**; 2 Header **B**:

1 Footer **A**; 2 Footer **B**:

These two choices allow you to use up to two headers and/or footers in a document at any given time. If you want alternating displays on even and odd pages, you can use the A definition for one set of pages and the B definition for alternate pages. If you are working with the same header or footer on every page, you can select either A or B for that display. After you have pressed **A** or **B** to name the header or footer you are creating, the following menu will appear at the bottom of your screen:

1 **D**iscontinue; 2 Every **P**age; 3 **O**dd Pages;
4 E**v**en Pages; 5 **E**dit

Select item 2 if you are using the same display on every page. Use 3 or 4 if you want a display to alternate pages. (Items 1 and 5 are used to change existing displays.) This will open a text editing screen that is similar to the document screen. Use this screen to create the text of the header or footer, then press F7 twice to return to your document. (The screen prompts you to use the Exit key—this is the WordPerfect name for the F7 key. You cannot exit from this screen by using the mouse.)

Including page numbers

To include page numbers as part of a header or footer, open a header or footer editing screen, then press Ctrl-B where you want the number to appear. This places a ^B symbol on screen. This symbol is replaced by the current page number when the document is printed.

Creating a header or footer places a code in your document at the current cursor position. A sample Header code is shown here:

```
[Header A:Odd pages;[Flsh Rgt]Chapter 1]
```

This code specifies the name (Header A), location (Odd pages), and contents (a right-aligned chapter title) of the header. Notice the Flush Right code that was inserted as part of the header. The Flush Right command (Alt-F6) and the Center command (Shift-F6) are particularly useful for positioning headers and footers where you want them. You can insert as many header or footer codes as you want in your document. The definition shown above for Header A will remain in effect until it is replaced by another Header A code.

Headers and footers do not appear on the document screen, but are visible when you use the View Document feature of the Print menu.

The following steps illustrate how to create a centered footer on every page that reads Page 1, Page 2, Page 3, etc.

1. Press Shift-F8 (or open the Layout menu), then select Page to open the Format: Page menu.

2. Select Footers, select Footer A, then select Every Page. This will open the footer text editing screen.

3. Press Shift-F6 for centered text, then type **Page**, press the Spacebar once, and then press Ctrl-B to insert the ^B symbol for page numbering.

4. Press F7 twice to return to the document screen. This screen will not show the footer you just created. Use the View Document feature (Shift-F7, V) to see the footer.

You can use WordPerfect's Block Copy commands to copy headers and footers from the document screen to the header/footer editing screen and also to copy entire headers or footers from one document to another.

Editing Existing Headers and Footers

It is possible to edit existing headers and footers after they have been created. To do this, press Shift-F8 (or open the Layout menu), select Page, select Header or Footer, press **A** or **B** to identify the header or footer you want to edit, then select Edit. The existing header or footer will be displayed on a text editing screen. Make the changes you desire and then press F7 twice to return to the document screen.

When you edit a header or footer, WordPerfect searches backwards from the current cursor position to find the header or footer code. If you have more than one code for any given header or footer name (e.g., you have two different definitions for Header A), place the cursor just after the code you want to edit to ensure that WordPerfect will find the correct code.

Placement of
Headers and Footers on a Page

WordPerfect places headers as close to the top margin as possible, but never places headers within the margin itself. This means that the first line of a header occupies the same part of a page that the first line of text would occupy if no header were present. WordPerfect automatically creates one blank line under a header and places the first line of text beneath that blank line. If you want to move a header to a higher position on the page, decrease the size of the top margin using the Format: Page menu (Shift-F8, P, M). If you want to increase the distance between the header and the top of the paper, insert hard returns at the top of your header when you create or edit it. If you want to increase the distance between a header and the subsequent text, add hard returns to the end of the header.

Like headers, footers are never placed within the margin of the page. Footers are placed just above the bottom margin. To move a footer lower on the page, decrease the size of the bottom margin (Shift-F8, P, M). The text above a footer is arranged so as to leave a blank line between the last line of text and the top of the footer. As with headers, you can adjust the distance between footers and the text by using hard returns.

Controlling Hyphenation

WordPerfect does not ordinarily hyphenate words when they are too long to fit on a line. In this Step, you will learn how to add hyphens, or dashes, to your documents, and how to control hyphen placement using either manual or automatic hyphenation features. You will also learn about WordPerfect's four different hyphen types, and when to use each type.

TURNING HYPHENATION ON AND OFF

To turn hyphenation on or off, press Shift-F8 (or open the Layout menu), select Line, and then select Hyphenation. (If you use letters to select menu items, notice that this option is chosen by pressing **Y**.) Select Yes to turn hyphenation on or No to turn it off, then press F7 or click the right mouse button to return to the document screen.

Turning hyphenation on inserts a **[Hyph On]** code at the current cursor position, and turning hyphenation off inserts a **[Hyph Off]** code. When you insert a **[Hyph On]** code, all subsequent text is hyphenated. If you turn hyphenation on before you type the text, any words that are too long for a line will be broken into two lines and hyphenated as you type. If you turn hyphenation on by inserting a **[Hyph On]** code in existing text, hyphenation takes place in all subsequent text when you move your cursor.

THE HYPHENATION PROMPT

When you turn hyphenation on, WordPerfect uses an online dictionary to determine hyphen position. If your document contains a word or name that is not in its dictionary, a hyphenation prompt appears that allows you to control where the hyphen should be placed. Figure 15.1 shows a document that was created without turning hyphenation on.

Figure 15.2 was created by returning the cursor to the beginning of the sample document and then turning hyphenation on. (If you want to recreate this document in order to practice hyphenation, use the default margins and use two spaces after periods.

```
Sometimes a typed word is too long to fit a line.  Word
hyphenation is a way to handle this kind of situation.  Some
names and words are not found in the hyphenation dictionary and
when this happens, you are given a prompt to respond to.  The
name Belserene is an example of one that is not in the
dictionary.
```

■ *Figure 15.1: A sample document with no hyphenation*

```
Sometimes a typed word is too long to fit a line.  Word hyphen-
ation is a way to handle this kind of situation.  Some names and
words are not found in the hyphenation dictionary and when this
happens, you are given a prompt to respond to.  The name Belser-
ene is an example of one that is not in the dictionary.
```

■ *Figure 15.2: The sample document after hyphenation*

However, because of differences in printer configurations, your document might not hyphenate like the one shown.) Figure 15.2 contains two examples of hyphenation: in the word "hyphenation" and in the name "Belserene." Because the word "hyphenation" is in its dictionary, WordPerfect hyphenates this word automatically. However, because the name "Belserene" is not in the dictionary, the following prompt is displayed after hyphenation is turned on:

`Position hyphen; Press ESC Belser-ene`

This prompt shows a suggested location for the hyphen. There are three ways to respond to a hyphenation prompt:

- Press Esc to accept the suggested hyphenation.

- Use ← and → to change the hyphen position, then press Esc to position a hyphen in the new location.

- Press F1 if you want the word to be wrapped to the next line without being hyphenated.

Hyphen-ation re-sponse options

CONTROLLING THE HYPHENATION PROMPT FREQUENCY

You can use the Setup command to change the Hyphenation Prompt frequency. To use this command, press Shift-F1 (or open the Files menu and select Setup), select Environment, then select Prompt for Hyphenation. You will see the following menu of choices on the status line:

`1 Never; 2 When Required; 3 Always`

If you select *Never*, hyphenation is entirely automatic. WordPerfect uses the hyphenation dictionary to position hyphens and, if a word is not in the dictionary, it wraps the entire word to the next line. *When Required* is the default option. If you select this option, prompts appear only for words that are not in the hyphenation dictionary. If you select *Always,* hyphenation is entirely manual. This means that the hyphenation prompt appears for every word that needs hyphenating.

TYPES OF HYPHENS

The hyphenation techniques just described place one kind of hyphen, called a *soft hyphen,* into your document. Soft hyphens alone can't handle all situations where hyphens are called for. In order to allow you greater flexibility, WordPerfect offers a total of four different hyphenation alternatives. These are: *soft hyphens, hard hyphens, hyphen characters,* and *invisible soft returns.*

Soft hyphens

Soft hyphens are hyphens that WordPerfect places in a document when you use the hyphenation procedures described above. These hyphens divide words that extend beyond the end of a line of text and appear as boldface dashes in the Reveal Codes display. If you reformat a document so that a word with a soft hyphen is no longer at the end of the line, the soft hyphen remains visible in the Reveal Codes display, but does not show up on the document screen and is not printed. If further reformatting again requires the use of a hyphen in the same word, the soft hyphen is used to determine where the hyphen should be placed, and it reappears in the word on the document screen.

Hard hyphens

Hard hyphens are dashes that you place in a document by pressing the hyphen character on the keyboard. These hyphens appear in the Reveal Codes display in boldface surrounded by square brackets (for example, sun[-]beaten). If you place a hard hyphen in a word that is too long to fit at the end of a line, WordPerfect hyphenates the word at the hard hyphen location. Unlike soft hyphens, however, hard hyphens remain visible in the document, and *are* printed if the text is later reformatted so that the word is located in the middle of a line. Use hard hyphens in compound words and names like "sun-beaten" and "Fong-Rodriguez," in which the hyphen is a permanent part of the expression.

Hyphen characters are used when you want to place dashes in a word and *don't* want the word to be hyphenated at that location. If, for example, you were typing a date in the form *mm-dd-yy* and did not want the date split onto two lines, you could use a hyphen character to ensure that the entire date would be wrapped to a new line if necessary. To enter a hyphen character, press Home and then the hyphen key in sequence. Hyphen characters appear as plain (rather than boldface) dashes in the Reveal Codes display.

Hyphen characters

Invisible soft returns are used for words or expressions that need to be divided without the use of a hyphen. For example, if you use an expression with a slash, such as "either/or," you might want the second part of the expression to be wrapped to the new line, but you would not want a hyphen added. To do this, you would place an invisible soft return at the point where the word or expression should be divided. The invisible soft return acts like a soft hyphen, but does not add a hyphen character where the word is divided. To enter an invisible soft return, press Home and then press Enter. Invisible soft returns do not appear in the document screen, and are shown as **[ISRT]** codes in the Reveal Codes display.

Invisible soft returns

EDITING HYPHENS

There may be times when you want to alter the hyphenation in a document after it has been set in order to improve the appearance of the final printed page. It is possible to remove hyphenation from a hyphenated word, to hyphenate a word that you previously indicated should not be hyphenated, or to change the position of an existing hyphen. All of these editing changes are most easily made with the Reveal Codes display visible.

Removing hyphen-ation

When you want to remove the hyphen from a hyphenated word, you need to add a Cancel Hyphenation code to the front of the word and then delete the hyphen. The Cancel Hyphenation code ([/]) is the same code that is entered in a document when you press F1 (Cancel) in response to a hyphenation prompt. To add this code manually, first display the Reveal Codes screen. Then move the cursor in the Reveal Codes window to the first letter of the word in question, then press Home and the slash key (/) in sequence. This will have no visible effect on the document screen, but will be visible as an added [/] code in the Reveal Codes screen. Once this code has been added, move the cursor to the hyphen character you want to remove and press Del.

Adding hyphen-ation

To hyphenate a word that has the Cancel Hyphenation code preceding it, you must first delete the [/] code. If hyphenation is on, WordPerfect hyphenates the word as soon as you move the cursor after deleting the code (either manually or automatically, depending on the hyphenation option you have selected).

Changing hyphen location

To change the position of a hyphen, you must set the Hyphenation Prompt option to Always (Shift-F1, E, 7). Next, delete the existing hyphen by highlighting the soft hyphen code in the Reveal Codes display and pressing Del. When you move the cursor after deleting the hyphen, WordPerfect beeps and displays the hyphenation prompt. Use ← or → to position the hyphen in a new location and press Esc to select the new hyphen location.

16

Creating Columns

■ ■ ■ ■ ■ ■ ■ ■ ■ ■ ■

This Step describes WordPerfect techniques for arranging text in columns. Creating columns in WordPerfect is a two-step process. First, you must define a column format. After you have defined a format, you must turn the columns feature on in order to arrange your text according to that format.

DEFINING A COLUMN FORMAT

Defining a column format involves the following options:

■ Selecting a column *type,* either *newspaper* or *parallel.*

■ Indicating how many columns you want on each page.

■ Setting a column arrangement by specifying the distance between columns and, if you want columns of different width, the width of each column.

You use the Text Column Definition menu shown in Figure 16.1 to set each of these aspects of column layout. To open the Text

Opening the Text Column Definition menu

Column Definition menu, press Alt-F7 (or open the Layout menu), select Columns, then select Define. Figure 16.1 shows the default settings for column arrangement. You can press F7 (or click the right mouse button) to accept these settings, or you can change any or all of the settings as described below.

Selecting a Column Type

Newspaper style columns

The most commonly used column type is newspaper style. Figure 16.2 illustrates a sample of text created using newspaper style columns. The text in newspaper columns flows down the length of one column and then continues to the top of the next.

Parallel columns

Figure 16.3 shows an example of parallel columns. In these columns, the flow of information moves across the page rather than down it. Text in the first column is paired horizontally with text in each subsequent column, and imaginary parallel lines mark the

```
Text Column Definition

    1 - Type                            Newspaper

    2 - Number of Columns               2

    3 - Distance Between Columns

    4 - Margins
       Column   Left    Right    Column   Left    Right
         1:      1"       4"        13:
         2:      4.5"     7.5"      14:
         3:                         15:
         4:                         16:
         5:                         17:
         6:                         18:
         7:                         19:
         8:                         20:
         9:                         21:
        10:                         22:
        11:                         23:
        12:                         24:

    Selection: 0
```

■ *Figure 16.1: The Text Column Definition menu*

```
                    NEWSPAPER COLUMNS

       Newspaper columns are de-        text were not arranged in col-
   signed   for   long,  continuous     umns.     Newspaper columns can
   blocks  of  text.  When  text  is    easily be set up either before
   arranged  in  this  format,   new    or after you have entered your
   lines   of   text  will  continue    text. Setting newspaper column
   within  the  same  column  until     format after the text has been
   the end of the page is reached.      entered can simplify many edit-
   Newspaper columns are ideal for      ing tasks.  In contrast, paral-
   magazines,    newspapers,   and      lel columns are far easier to
   newsletters.     These  publica-     work with if you set up your
   tions use small type sizes that      columns  before  you  start  to
   would  be  difficult  to  read  if   type.
```

- *Figure 16..2: Newspaper style columns*

```
                    PARALLEL COLUMNS

   Newspaper          1 or N    The flow of text goes down the column
                                until the bottom of the column has
                                been reached.  At this point, text
                                continues at the top of the next
                                column.

   Parallel           2 or P    The flow of text moves across the
                                page in related blocks of material.
                                Each block of material can be of
                                variable length.  Text will wrap
                                within a column until you use the
                                Hard Page command to move to the next
                                column across.

   Parallel with      3 or B    The flow of text is the same as with
   Block Protect                regular parallel columns, but all
                                horizontally related sections of text
                                must remain on a single page.
```

- *Figure 16.3: Parallel columns*

top of each group of columns. WordPerfect allows you to choose
between two forms of parallel columns: with and without Block
Protect. When Block Protect is on, horizontally related sections of
text must all be contained on a single page.

To select a column type, display the Text Column Definition
menu on screen, then select Type. This will display the following

menu of choices:

1 **N**ewspaper; **2** **P**arallel; **3** Parallel with **B**lock
Protect

Use this menu to select the column style you want. The cursor
will then return to the Selection prompt, allowing you to set other
aspects of column design. See "Strategies for Arranging Text in
Columns" below for more information about working with newspaper and parallel columns.

Setting the Number of Columns

By default, WordPerfect sets the number of columns on a page to
two. To change this setting, display the Text Column Definition
menu on screen, then select Number of Columns. Type in the
number of columns you want, then press Enter. When you do this,
WordPerfect automatically calculates the proper spacing for that
number of equal-width columns, with as close as possible to one-
half inch between columns. You can change the distance between
columns and margins and/or the column widths by using the last
two items on the Text Column Definition menu.

Distance between Columns

The default distance between columns is one-half inch (0.5"). To
change this setting, display the Text Column Definition menu on
screen, then select Distance Between Columns. Type in the distance you want between column margins and press Enter. When
you change the value for Distance Between Columns, WordPerfect will automatically adjust the column margins to reflect the
new setting.

Setting Column Margins Manually

Use the Margins option of the Text Column Definition menu when you want to create columns of unequal width. This feature allows you to give specific measurements for the left and right margins of each column on the page. When you use this feature, WordPerfect does *not* automatically set a distance between columns, so be sure to take this distance into account when you plan your margin settings. Always select the number of columns you want before you set column margins with the Margins option.

To set column margins manually, display the Text Column Definition menu on screen, then select Margins. This will move the cursor to the left margin setting of the first column. Type in a measurement for this margin and press Enter. The cursor will move to the right margin setting. Continue entering new margin settings and pressing Enter until all margins have been adjusted.

TURNING
THE COLUMN FORMAT ON AND OFF

Once you have selected the desired column settings, you must still turn the columns feature on. Until you do this, WordPerfect continues to arrange text across the full page. When you press F7 (or click the right mouse button) to exit from the Text Definition menu, WordPerfect displays the Columns menu shown here:

Exiting from the Text Column Definition menu

```
Columns: 1 On; 2 Off; 3 Define
```

If you want the column arrangement to begin at the current cursor location, select On from this menu. Doing this will turn columns on and return you to the document screen. If you don't want to turn columns on immediately after creating a column definition, press F7 when the Columns menu appears on screen. If you do this, you can turn Columns on at any subsequent location in your document by pressing Alt-F7 (or opening the Layout menu), selecting Columns, then selecting On.

By creating a column definition and turning the column feature on, you place two codes in your document. The first code is a column definition code such as this one:

```
[Col Def:Newspaper;2;1",4";4.5",7.5"]
```

This code identifies the column type, the number of columns, and the left and right margin settings for each column on a page. The second code is a [Col On] code that turns that column definition on. Like all WordPerfect codes, these codes are saved as part of your document.

If you want to return to ordinary text display after creating columns of text, turn the columns feature off by pressing Alt-F7 (or opening the Layout menu), selecting Columns, then selecting Off. This inserts a [Col Off] code at the current cursor position. Text below a column off code is not arranged in columns.

You can turn column mode on and off as frequently as you want in a document, using as many different column definition codes as you desire. Each time you turn the column feature on, WordPerfect creates columns using the preceding column definition code.

STRATEGIES FOR ARRANGING TEXT IN COLUMNS

If you are working with newspaper columns, you can set your column layout either before or after you have typed your text. Typing in the text first is often desirable, because cursor movement and text editing are easier before the text has been arranged in columns.

To add columns to existing text, move the cursor to the point where you want the column format to begin, then define your column format (Alt-F7) and turn columns on. The text that follows will be rearranged into column format as soon as you use any of WordPerfect's cursor control commands. (If you have a slow machine, you may have to wait a few seconds before the columns appear.) Where text fills one column and moves to the next column, WordPerfect inserts a soft page code ([**SPg**]). If you subsequently delete the [**Col On**] code, the text returns to its original arrangement, and the soft page codes that have been added to the document are automatically removed.

Adding columns to existing text

You can also create newspaper columns by defining and turning on the columns before you start to type. As you type, material automatically arranges itself in columns, with a [**SPg**] code at the end of each column.

If you want to begin a new column before you fill the current column, use the Hard Page command (Ctrl-Enter). When the columns feature is on, pressing Ctrl-Enter moves the cursor to the top of the next column and inserts a hard page code ([**HPg**]) at the bottom of the current column. (If the cursor is in the last column of one page, pressing Ctrl-Enter moves it to the top of the first column on the next page.) If you subsequently remove the [**Col On**] code, any hard page codes you have entered remain in your document, and, as a result, these codes start new pages rather than new columns.

Starting a new column with Ctrl-Enter

Unlike newspaper columns, parallel columns should always be defined and turned on *before* you type the text. Once you have turned on the parallel column format, text fills the first column until you insert a hard page code by pressing Ctrl-Enter. At this point, the cursor moves to the next column, ready to start a new line that is even with the top of the material in the previous column. The Hard Page command continues to have this effect until

Entering text in parallel columns

you reach the last column on the page. When you press Ctrl-Enter at this point, the cursor moves back to the first column, positioned so that there is a blank line between the new cursor position and the longest section of text in the set of columns above it. In order to do this, WordPerfect adds three codes to your document: [Col Off], [HRt], and [Col On]. If you don't want the blank line between sets of columns, you can delete the [HRt] code in this sequence.

COLUMNS AND CURSOR MOVEMENT

If you have a mouse, you will find it easiest to move the cursor through a document that is arranged in columns by using your mouse. Mouse cursor movement is not affected in any way by columns. Simply move the mouse cursor to the desired location and click the left mouse button.

If you are using the keyboard to move the cursor, you can move the cursor within a column as you ordinarily would. Use the following techniques to move from column to column:

- Press Ctrl-Home followed by → to move the cursor one column to the right.

- Press Ctrl-Home followed by ← to move the cursor one column to the left.

When you are working with columns turned on, a new indicator *(Col 1, Col 2,* and so on) is added to the status line just in front of the document number. This indicator changes as you move from column to column.

Changing
Default Settings

■ ■ ■ ■ ■ ■ ■ ■ ■ ■ ■

This Step describes how to use the Set-up menu to change a variety of default settings. These include: changing the initial page-formatting features, changing menu display options, changing the units of measure you use for page formatting, controlling the automatic backup of files, and adjusting your mouse set up.

CHANGING INITIAL PAGE-FORMATTING FEATURES

By default, WordPerfect creates documents using a one-inch margin at each side of the page. The right margin is justified and tab settings are placed at every half inch. If you routinely create documents that use a different page-formatting arrangement, you can change these initial settings.

To change the initial page-formatting settings, press Shift-F1 (or open the File menu and select Setup), select Initial Settings, and then select Initial Codes. This will display the Initial Codes editing screen, which resembles a document screen except that, in this screen, the Reveal Codes display is always visible and there is a prompt that reads *Press **Exit** when done*. Use the Initial Settings editing screen to define new default conditions by inserting appropriate formatting codes, just as you would if you were modifying an individual document. For example, if you like a non-justified right margin, you can insert a **[Just: Left]** code by using the Format: Line menu (Shift-F8, 2).

When you have added all the codes you want to the Initial Codes editing screen, return to the document screen by pressing F7 twice.

Codes that you insert using the Setup menu will be in effect in all subsequent documents, but will not be displayed in the Reveal Codes display. Documents that you have already created will not be affected by the new codes. You can override any of the initial codes by inserting new codes into individual documents.

CHANGING MENU OPTIONS

You can also use the Setup menu to change a variety of menu display options. These changes are made with the Setup: Menu Options menu shown in Figure 17.1. To display this menu, press Shift-F1 (or open the File menu and select Setup), select Display, and then select Menu Options. You can use options 1, 2, 3, 5, and 6 to change the onscreen appearance of different WordPerfect menus.

You can also use the Setup: Menu Options menu to change the pull-down menu bar display. If you would like the menu bar to be visible at all times, select Menu Bar Remains Visible, and then select Yes. If you would like to be able to display the pull-down

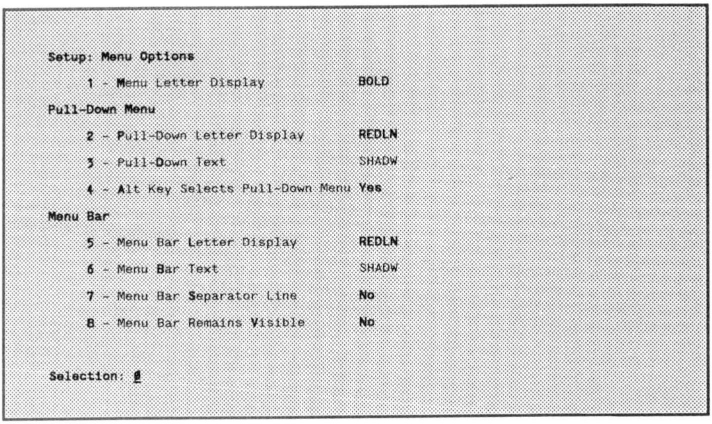

■ *Figure 17.1: The Setup: Menu Options menu*

menu bar by pressing the Alt key alone (rather than using Alt-=), select Alt Key Selects Pull-Down Menu, and then select Yes.

CHANGING UNITS OF MEASURE

By default, WordPerfect uses inches to measure positions on the page. If you prefer, you can change this measurement option using the Setup: Units of Measure menu shown in Figure 17.2. To display this menu, press Shift-F1 (or open the File menu and select Setup), select Environment, and then select Units of Measure.

Pull-down menu bar display options

The Units of Measure menu allows you to select the units of measure you use for page-formatting commands, such as setting margins and tabs (option 1), and also the units used for the Status Line Display (option 2). To change units of measure, select the measurement option you want to change, and then enter the letter or symbol that corresponds to the measurement system you want to use. Use either the letter **i** or the inch symbol (") to select

Changing Default Settings **119**

```
Setup: Units of Measure
    1 - Display and Entry of Numbers          *
            for Margins, Tabs, etc.

    2 - Status Line Display                   *

Legend:

    * = inches
    i = inches
    c = centimeters
    p = points
    w = 1200ths of an inch
    u = WordPerfect 4.2 Units (Lines/Columns)




Selection: _
```

■ *Figure 17.2: The Setup: Units of Measure menu*

inches. Use the letter **c** to select centimeters. Use the letter **p** to select points. (There are 72 points in an inch. Use the letter **w** to select a unit equal to 1/1200 of an inch. Use the letter **u** to select WordPerfect 4.2 units. (In this measurement system, one unit is equal to the width of one character if you are moving across the page, and the length of one line if you are moving down the page. This measurement system was used with earlier versions of WordPerfect.)

Any measurement value you enter *without indicating units* will automatically be assumed to be in the currently selected units, if you *do* specify other units (using c, p, w, or u), WordPerfect will recognize these units and automatically calculate and display the equivalent measurement using the currently selected units. For example, if you have selected inches as the current units for display and entry of numbers, and then set a margin in the Format: Line menu by typing **72p**, WordPerfect will enter this setting as **1"**.

AUTOMATIC FILE BACKUP OPTIONS

WordPerfect includes two automatic back-up options that you can use to help you avoid accidentally losing important material: Timed Document Backup and Original Document Backup. To choose either of these options, use the Setup: Backup menu shown in Figure 17.3. To open this menu, press Shift-F1 (or open the File menu and select Setup), select Environment, and then select Backup Options.

Timed Document Backup

When the Timed Document Backup option is set to Yes, WordPerfect automatically makes backup copies of your files. Use the Minutes Between Backups item to specify how frequently you want backup copies to be made. As you work, the document or documents you have on screen are saved to a temporary file each time the specified interval of time elapses. The backup file is named WP{WP}.BK1 for a document in the Doc 1 screen and WP{WP}.BK2 for a document in the Doc 2 screen. These files remain on your disk as long as you are working in WordPerfect,

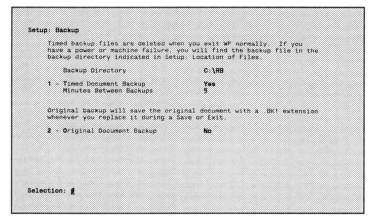

Figure 17.3: The Setup: Backup menu

and also if you *do not* exit properly from WordPerfect (as would be the case in a power interruption). *They are deleted from your disk if you exit WordPerfect properly.*

Use the Setup command to select a directory for the temporary backup files. Press Shift-F1 (or open the File menu and select Setup), select Location of Files, select Backup Files, and then type the directory path you want these files to be stored in, and press Enter. (For example, type **C:\PRACTICE** if you want the backup files to be saved to the PRACTICE directory.)

If power is interrupted before you exit from WordPerfect, you will see the following prompt when you reenter WordPerfect:

```
Are other copies of WordPerfect currently
running? (Y/N)
```

Original Document Backup

Press **N** to respond to this question. This will return you to the WordPerfect document screen. You can then retrieve your backup files from the directory you specified with the Setup menu. (If you did not specify a directory for the timed backup files, they will be saved in the directory that contains your WordPerfect program, and you will be prompted to rename the files after you press **N** in response to the question shown above.)

When the Original Document Backup option is set to Yes, WordPerfect automatically creates a backup file each time you re-place a previously saved file with an updated version of that file. This allows you to retrieve material from the most recently saved version of the file by opening the backup file. The replaced version of the file is saved with the same file name as the document you are working with, but with a .BK! file extension. For example, files named SMITH, SMITH.LTR, or SMITH.JAN would all be backed up to the same file, called SMITH.BK!. The backup file would be replaced each time you saved any of the SMITH files.

Original Document Backup files are automatically saved to the directory that contains the original document. These files are not deleted when you exit from WordPerfect.

Although these two backup options can help reduce the likelihood of inadvertently losing material, they *do not* cover all possible circumstances when information might be lost. For instance, if you exit from WordPerfect properly and later discover that you cannot use the disk on which you saved your document, neither of WordPerfect's backup options would help you retrieve that information.

USING THE MOUSE MENU

If you are using a mouse, you can use the Setup: Mouse menu to control a variety of mouse installation features. The Setup: Mouse menu is shown in Figure 17.4. To open this menu, press Shift-F1 (or open the File menu and select Setup), and then select Mouse.

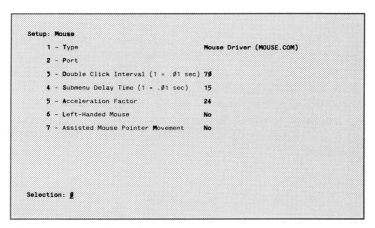

■ *Figure 17.4: The Setup: Mouse menu*

STEP

17

Selecting a mouse driver

Use the Type option of the Setup: Mouse menu to select the mouse driver that WordPerfect will use to control your mouse. When you select this option, WordPerfect displays a list of mouse drivers. Highlight the driver that corresponds to the mouse you are using and press Enter to select that driver. The default selection is Mouse Driver (MOUSE.COM). (When you use this driver, you must run the mouse driver program before entering WordPerfect. When you select any other mouse driver, you can use your mouse whenever you use WordPerfect without running any additional programs.)

Selecting a serial mouse port

Use the Port option if you are using a serial mouse and want to select the appropriate serial port for your mouse. When you select this option, WordPerfect displays a menu of four possible ports, Com 1 through Com 4.

You can also use the Mouse menu to change the settings of a variety of features that control the way WordPerfect responds to your mouse. These include: the interval that distinguishes a double click from two individual clicks (Double Click Interval); the way a mouse can be used for displaying pull-down menus (Submenu Delay Time); how sensitive the mouse pointer is to actual mouse movement (Acceleration Factor); an option for reversing the role of mouse buttons (Left-handed Mouse); and an option that automatically moves the mouse cursor to the menu bar, or any menu that is displayed on the status line, rather than leaving it in its current position (Assisted Mouse Pointer Movement). For more information about how to set these features, refer to WordPerfect's online help (F3).

Macros and
Other Shortcuts

In this Step, you will learn how to use WordPerfect features that are designed to help you streamline your work. These include both built-in features for saving keystrokes, as well as user-defined shortcuts known as macros.

SHORTCUTS FOR SAVING KEYSTROKES
WordPerfect's built-in shortcuts include a method of repeating any keystroke a specified number of times, and a method for entering the current date into a document without having to type that date.

Using the Esc Key for Repeated Keystrokes
You can use the Esc key anytime you need to enter the same keystroke several times in a row. When you press the Esc key, the following prompt appears on the status line:

```
Repeat Value = 8
```

(The number following *Repeat Value* may not be the default, 8, if the repetition number has already been changed as described below.) At this point, any keystroke you enter will automatically be repeated eight times. To insert a row of eight asterisks, you would press Esc and then press *. You can also use the Esc key to speed up editing and cursor control. For example, to delete eight characters, you can press Esc, then Del. (Note that Esc, Backspace does not have the same result as Esc, Del.) To move the cursor eight lines down, you can press Esc and then ↓.

Changing the repetition number

If you want to change to a new repetition number, type that value when you see the *Repeat Value* prompt. (The existing number will disappear as soon as you type a new one.) If you press Enter at this point, the Repeat Value prompt will disappear, but the new value will remain in effect each time you press Esc until you exit from WordPerfect. If you do not press Enter after you change the repetition number, but instead press a keystroke, that keystroke will be repeated using the new repetition number. When you do this, the repetition number returns to the default value next time you press Esc.

Changing the default repetition number

To change the default repetition number, press Shift-F1 (or open the File menu and select Setup), then select Initial Settings. This opens the Setup: Initial Settings menu. Select Repeat Value, enter a new repetition number, then press F7 (or click the right mouse button) to return to your document.

Entering Dates into a Document

WordPerfect allows you to enter the current date into your document without having to type it out. There are two options you can use to insert dates with this feature: *Text* and *Code*. When you insert a date using the Text option, the current date (as it was logged into your system's memory when you turned on your computer) is entered into your document exactly as if you had typed it manually. When you insert a date using the Code option, WordPerfect displays and prints the date as if it had been typed as text, but on later dates when you open the same document, the coded date will change to reflect the current date. For example, if you insert a date on January 1 using the Code option, the date will automatically change to January 2 if you open the document the next day (or if you reset the current date in your computer system).

To enter a date at the current cursor position, press Shift-F5 (or open the Tools menu) and then select Date Text or Date Code to select the option you want.

By default, dates are displayed using the full month name followed by the date, a comma, and then the full year (for example, March 1, 1992). Use the Date Format menu to change this format. To display this menu, press Shift-F5 (or open the Tools menu), then select Date Format. This menu lists code characters that you can use to change the format for the month, day, and year, as well as codes that you can use if you want to include the day of the week and/or the time. Use these codes to enter the date in the format you want. When you enter the codes, include spaces, commas, and so on where you want them. There are several examples given on the menu that you can use as models. After you have entered a new format, press F7 (or click the right mouse button) twice to return to the document screen. Doing this affects the way subsequent dates are inserted, but does not affect any dates you have already inserted in any of your documents.

Changing the date format

WORKING WITH MACROS

A macro is a prerecorded sequence of keystrokes that you can retrieve at any time without having to repeat the entire sequence. WordPerfect macros can include text characters, command keystrokes, or any combination of the two. It is also possible to create

macros that pause to allow you to enter information that changes
each time you use the macro.

Defining a Macro

To define a macro, press Ctrl-F10 (or open the Tools menu, select
Macro, then select Define). The following prompt will appear on
the status line:

`Define Macro:`

Use this prompt to name the macro you are about to define. You
can name a macro in either of two ways. You can type in a name
that is no more than eight letters long and then press Enter, or you
can name it by holding down the Alt key and pressing a letter key.
(The way you name a macro determines how you will execute that
macro later.)

After you name the macro, the following prompt appears:

`Description:`

You can type an optional short macro description and press Enter
in response to this prompt, or you can press Enter alone if you
choose to omit the description. (Macro descriptions are visible
only when you use the macro editing screen, a feature not covered
in this book.)

When you have responded to the *Description:* prompt, the status
line will contain a flashing prompt that reads:

`Macro Def`

When this prompt is visible, any keystroke you press will be recorded as part of the macro. These keystrokes will also be entered
into the document that is on screen when you define the macro.

To conclude your macro definition, press Ctrl-F10 again (or open the Tools menu, select Macro, then select Define) when you have completed the sequence of keystrokes that you want to record.

Canceling a macro definition

You can cancel a Macro Define command using the F1 (Cancel) key *only until the flashing* Macro Def *prompt appears.* Once this flashing prompt is visible, the Cancel command is incorporated as part of the macro keystroke sequence. The only way to interrupt the macro-definition process once the flashing *Macro Def* prompt appears is to repeat the Ctrl-F10 command (or repeat the pull-down menu commands) in order to complete the macro. If you want, you can then repeat the macro definition process from the beginning in order to replace the incorrect version you just created. If you redefine a macro using the same name, you will have to confirm that you want to replace the existing version of that macro.

The following exercise demonstrates how to create a short macro that inserts formatting commands, but adds no text to a document. The macro you create here can be executed any time you want to type a nonjustified, double-spaced manuscript. In this example, the macro is named using the Alt key option.

1. Begin with a clear document screen. Press Ctrl-F10 to begin defining the macro.

2. Press Alt-m in response to the *Define Macro:* prompt in order to name the macro.

3. Press Enter in response to the *Description:* prompt to omit the macro description. After you do this, the *Macro Def* message will flash on the status line. You are now ready to record a sequence of keystrokes.

4. To turn the right justification off, press Shift-F8 (or open the Layout menu), select Line, select Justification, then select Left.

5. With the Format: Line menu still visible, select Line Spacing, then type **2** for double spacing, and press Enter.

6. Press F7 or click the right mouse button to return to the document. Notice that the *Macro Def* message is still flashing.

7. Press Ctrl-F10 to complete the macro. The flashing message will disappear. Use the Reveal Codes command (Alt-F3) to see the two codes that you just created.

Executing a Macro

Once you have defined a macro, you can repeat the recorded sequence of keystrokes at any time by executing that macro. The technique you use to execute a macro depends upon the method you used for naming the macro.

Executing macros with the Macro command

If you gave a macro a full name, press Alt-F10 (or open the Tools menu, select Macro, and then select Execute) to execute that macro. This will bring the following prompt to the status line:

    Macro:

In response to this prompt, type the name of the macro and press Enter. This will initiate the series of keystrokes you entered when you defined that macro.

Executing macros using the Alt key

If you named a macro by pressing the Alt key and a letter key, you can invoke that macro by repeating this same keystroke combination (*without* pressing Alt-F10 or opening the Tools menu).

To execute the macro you created in the previous exercise, begin with a clear document screen that contains no formatting codes.

Display the Reveal Codes Screen. (If the codes you entered when you created the macro are still on screen, clear the screen by pressing F7, N, N.) Press Alt-m to execute the macro. The two formatting codes that are included in this macro should appear in the Reveal Codes display.

Macro Files

Macros are saved on your disk as files with a .WPM extension. When you use the full-name option for naming macros, the .WPM extension is added to the name that you enter when you create the macro. When you use the Alt-key option, WordPerfect uses the names ALTA.WPM, ALTB.WPM, ALTC.WPM, and so on.

Use the Setup: Location of Files menu to select a location for your macro files. To display this menu, press Shift-F1 (or open the Files menu and select Setup), then select Location of Files. Select the Keyboard/Macro Files option, type a directory path for your macro files (for example, C:\WP51), press Enter, and then press F7 to return to the document screen. If you prefer to have all macros available at all times, save these files to the same directory that contains the WordPerfect program (usually C:\WP51). This is a desirable location for general-purpose macros. Macros saved to other drives or directories will be available only when you are working in those drives or directories. If you do not specify any directory path for your macro files, WordPerfect will save them to the currently logged drive or directory, and they will be available only from that drive or directory.

Selecting a directory for macro files

You can delete macros from any directory by using the List Files command (F5, Enter), highlighting the macro name, selecting Delete from the List Files menu, then selecting Yes to confirm that you want to delete the file.

Using
macros
from
previous
versions
of WP

If you are upgrading from WordPerfect 5.0 to WordPerfect 5.1, you do not need to redefine or convert macros, provided that the keystroke combinations for the commands in those macros have not changed. You can also use version 5.1 macros with version 5.0 if you have not incorporated any of the new features of the more recent version.

Creating Macros that Pause for Input

It is sometimes convenient to make macros that can adjust to a particular situation by pausing for input. For example, it is possible to create a macro for preparing memos that types in the word **TO:**, moves to the correct tab position, and then waits for input before continuing with **FROM:**, and so on.

The basic procedure for creating macros that pause for input is the same as that described above. Use the Macro Define command, name and describe your macro, and then enter a sequence of commands. When you reach a point in a macro where you want it to pause for input, press Ctrl-PgUp. This displays the following menu of options:

1 Pause; **2** Display; **3** Assign; **4** Comment

Select Pause from this menu, then type in a sample entry. This sample entry will be added to the current document on screen, but will not be saved as a permanent part of the macro. Press Enter when you have completed the sample entry. (No **[HRt]** code will be entered at this point. In this situation, pressing the Enter key simply indicates the end of user input and the continuation of the macro.) You can then continue entering your macro keystrokes as usual.

The exercise that follows creates the document shown in Figure 18.1. This macro demonstrates the use of the pause feature. It

18

```
Date:      February 10, 1992

From:      John Smith

-----------------------------------------------------------
```

- *Figure 18.1: A macro that pauses for input*

also demonstrates the use of the Esc key and the automatic date-entering feature. The macro types **Date:** and then enters the date automatically as text. The cursor is moved down to the third line, and the macro pauses for input after typing **From:**. Finally, the cursor moves down and the macro creates a row of dashes.

To create the macro shown in Figure 18.1:

1. Begin with a clear document screen. Press Ctrl-F10 to define the macro.

2. To name the macro, type **memo** and press Enter in response to the *Define Macro:* prompt. Press Enter again in response to the *Description:* prompt to omit the macro description. You should now see the flashing *Macro Def* message.

3. Type **Date:** and then press the Tab key.

4. Press Shift-F5, then select Date Text to enter the current date as text.

5. Press Enter twice to move the cursor to the beginning of the third line.

6. Type **From:** and then press the Tab key.

7. Press Ctrl-PgUp, and then select Pause from the resulting menu.

8. Type **Jane Doe** and press Enter. (Notice that this Enter indicates the end of the sample input and does not move the cursor.)

Macros and Other Shortcuts **133**

9.   Press Enter twice. These two hard returns move the cursor down two lines.

10. Press Esc, type **65** (without pressing Enter), then press the hyphen key (-) to enter a line of 65 dashes.

11. Press Ctrl-F10 to complete the macro definition.

To invoke this macro:

1.   Clear the screen without saving your work (F7, N, N).

2.   Press Alt-F10, then type **memo** and press Enter in response to the *Macro:* prompt.

3.   The macro will automatically type **Date:**, enter the current date, and move the cursor down two lines. Then, after it types **From:**, the macro will pause. At this point, type **John Smith** and press Enter. Once you have provided this input, execution of the macro will continue automatically, and the final document should look like Figure 18.1.

Working with Fonts

This Step covers techniques for varying the typeface style, or font, that you use in your WordPerfect documents. You will learn how to determine which fonts are supported by your printer, how to add additional fonts to your system, and finally, how to select the fonts you want to use for any given section of text.

ADDING FONTS TO YOUR SYSTEM

Fonts can be included in a personal computer system in one of three ways: They may be *resident* in your printer, or they may be added by using either *cartridges* or *soft fonts*. Resident fonts are those that have been built into your printer. No installation procedures are necessary in order to use resident fonts in your WordPerfect documents. Font cartridges are small hardware additions that you can snap into cartridge slots in some printers. Cartridge fonts, once installed, are available as soon as a printer is turned on. Soft fonts are added to your system by means of additional software. Soft fonts must be sent to the printer and stored in its memory each time you turn it on. This process is called *downloading.*

Listing available fonts

To find out what fonts are ready for use with the printer you have installed, press Ctrl-F8 (or open the Font menu), then select Base Font. This displays the Base Font menu, which lists the currently available fonts. The currently selected font is highlighted and marked with an asterisk.

Sizing fonts

If a selection on the list is listed as *scalable,* it means that you can use that selection to create fonts of different sizes. If the font is followed by a size indicator, it means that the selection can only be used for that font size. Sizes are given in either *points* (1/72") or *cpi* (characters per inch). Point measurements for fonts indicate the vertical distance from the top of the tallest letter of the font to the bottom of the letter that descends furthest down. Character-per-inch measurements are only given for fonts in which all characters are of uniform width. (Unlike point measurements, cpi measurements decrease as the size of the font increases.)

Press F1 to return to the document screen from the Base Font menu without making any changes to the currently selected font.

INSTALLING FONT CARTRIDGES

Install your font cartridges by snapping them into place before you turn on your printer. Once you have installed a cartridge, you must let WordPerfect know which cartridge you have installed. To do this, press Shift-F7 (or open the File menu and select Print), choose Select Printer, check to see that the printer you are working with is highlighted, select Edit, select Cartridges and Fonts, highlight Cartridges (using ↓ and ↑), and then press Enter. This will display a list of cartridges that are available for your printer.

Highlight the name of the cartridge you installed (using ↓ and ↑), and then type an asterisk (*) in order to select that cartridge. (You can remove an asterisk by highlighting the marked file and pressing either * or Del.) Press F7 five times (or click the right mouse button five times) to return to the document screen.

INSTALLING SOFT FONTS

In order to create a library of soft font files on your hard disk, you will need to follow the instructions that come with your soft font program. Once this is done, you must work with WordPerfect to complete the installation process. This involves two steps: telling WordPerfect which directory contains your soft font files and specifying which fonts from your font library you want to use.

To specify a directory for your soft fonts, press Shift-F7 (or open the File menu and select Print), choose Select Printer, check to see that the printer you are working with is highlighted, select Edit, choose Path for Downloadable Fonts and Printer Command Files, then type the directory path that contains your library of font files (for example, C:\PCLFONTS), and press Enter. Press F7 (or click the right mouse button) three times to return to the document screen.

Specifying a directory for soft fonts

The next step is to tell WordPerfect which fonts you want to make available to the printer. This step is necessary because your printer has a limited memory capacity and each soft font occupies printer memory. You can't work with more soft fonts at one time than your printer memory will allow.

Specifying the fonts you want to work with

To specify which fonts you want to work with, press Shift-F7 (or open the File menu and select Print), choose Select Printer, check to see that the printer you are working with is highlighted, select

Edit, select Cartridges and Fonts, highlight Soft Fonts (using ↓ and ↑), and then press Enter. (Depending on your printer, you may now see a list of font groups that includes the soft fonts you have added to your system and other font groups that are available for your printer from the manufacturer. If this screen is displayed, highlight the soft font group that you want to work with and press Enter.) You should now see the Select Printer: Soft Fonts screen. This screen is used for marking the fonts you want to work with.

Marking fonts

There are three ways of marking fonts on the Select Printer: Soft Fonts screen—with a plus sign (+), with an asterisk (*), or with both symbols. The way you mark a font determines when and how it is downloaded to your printer.

Marking fonts with +

A font marked with a plus sign (+) is only downloaded to the printer if you are printing a document that calls for that particular font. You can mark as many fonts as you want with this symbol, and doing so is the easiest way to ensure that all fonts are available at all times. However, when you print documents using fonts marked in this way, you must wait for all needed fonts to be downloaded *each* time you print a document.

Marking fonts with *

Fonts marked with an asterisk (*) are downloaded to the printer only if you *initialize* the printer (see below), and these fonts remain in your printer's memory until the printer is turned off or reinitialized. When you mark a font with an asterisk, a display in the upper-right corner of the screen indicates how much printer memory is still available. WordPerfect won't let you mark more fonts than you can download to your printer at any one time.

Marking fonts with *+

Fonts marked with both an asterisk and a plus sign (*+), like those marked only with an asterisk, are downloaded to your printer when you initialize it. However, WordPerfect will automatically unload a font marked in this way if additional printer memory is needed for a new print job.

To mark fonts on the soft fonts list, you can use PgDn, PgUp, ↑, and ↓ to highlight the font you want to mark. When the font is highlighted, press either * or + to mark it. (You can delete symbols by repeating the keystrokes you used to mark them, or by pressing the Del key.) Use F7 (or click the right mouse button) to exit from the font selection screen. After you have marked the fonts you want, return to the document screen, press F7 (or click the right mouse button) until the document screen reappears.

*Marking fonts with *,+*

If you have marked soft fonts with an asterisk, you must initialize the printer before you can use them. To do this, press Shift-F7 (or open the File menu and select Print), then select Initialize Printer. WordPerfect will display the following prompt:

Initializing the printer

```
Proceed with Printer Initialization? No (Yes)
```

Select Yes in response to this prompt. You will be returned to the document screen while the fonts you marked with an asterisk are downloaded to the printer. You can work on your document and send print commands while this occurs, but no jobs will be printed until initialization is complete.

SELECTING FONTS
FOR YOUR DOCUMENTS

There are two ways to select fonts for your WordPerfect documents; you can either change the *base font* (using one of three available methods) or you can change *attributes* (such as size or italics) of the currently selected base font.

Changing the Base Font

There are three ways to change the base font in a WordPerfect document: with the Font command, the Format command, or the Print command.

Using the Font command

The most flexible method of selecting a base font is with the Font command. When you select a font with this command, a code identifying the selected font is inserted in your document at the current cursor position. (The exact font name given in the code depends on the type of fonts you have installed in your system.) The font you selected will be used for all subsequent text until you insert a new base font code in the document.

To insert a Base Font code, press Ctrl-F8 (or open the Font menu), then select Base Font. Use the arrow keys to highlight the font you want from the resulting list, then press Enter. If you select a scalable font, you will see the prompt

    Point Size:

followed by the point size of the currently selected font. Type in a new font size (if you wish) and press Enter to complete the font selection. This will return you to the document screen. Nonscalable fonts of different sizes are each listed individually. If you select a nonscalable font, the point size prompt does not appear, and you will be returned to the document screen as soon as you press Enter after highlighting the font.

Figure 19.1 shows the Reveal Codes display for a document with two base font codes that have been inserted with the Font command. Notice that the presence of these codes does not affect the appearance of text on the document screen. To see the effect of a Font command, you must use the View Document command (Shift-F7, V). Figure 19.2 shows the View Document screen for the document in Figure 19.1.

Using the Format command

You can also select base fonts using the Format command. This command changes the initial base font for an entire document. No code is inserted, and your cursor can be anywhere when you invoke the command. The font you choose is saved as part of the document.

```
Changing Base Font

The heading of this document uses a 36 point Times
Roman Bold font.  The text of this paragraph uses a 20
point Times Roman italic font.  The different fonts can
be seen with the View Document feature, but not in the
ordinary document screen.




C:\UR51\E\FIG17-1.WP                        Doc 1 Pg 1 Ln 1" Pos 1"
(                                                    )
[Font:CG Times Bold (Scalable) 36pt]Changing Base Font[HRt]
[HRt]
[Font:CG Times Italic (Scalable) 20pt]The heading of this document uses a 36 poi
nt Times[SRt]
Roman Bold font.  The text of this paragraph uses a 20[SRt]
point Times Roman italic font.  The different fonts can[SRt]
be seen with the View Document feature, but not in the[SRt]
ordinary document screen.


Press Reveal Codes to restore screen
```

■ *Figure 19.1: A document containing base font codes*

To select an initial base font with the Format command, press Shift-F8 (or open the Layout menu), select Document, then select Initial Base Font. Highlight the font you want and press Enter. (If you select a scalable font, type in the point size you want and press Enter to complete the font selection.) Press F7 (or click the right mouse button) to return to the document screen.

Font selections made with the Font command override an initial font selection made with the Format command.

Using the Print command

You can use the print command to make a permanent change in the default base font for all subsequent documents. To do this, press Shift-F7 (or open the File menu and select Print), choose Select Printer, check to be sure the printer you are working with is highlighted, select Edit, select Initial Base Font, highlight the font you want, and then press Enter. (If you select a scalable font, type in the point size you want and press Enter to complete the font selection.) Press F7 (or click the right mouse button) three times to return to the document screen.

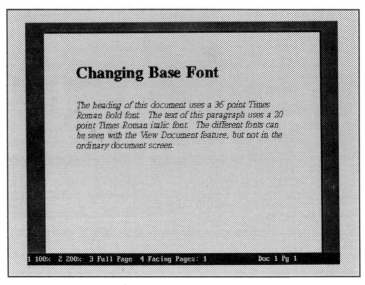

Changing Base Font

The heading of this document uses a 36 point Times
Roman Bold font. The text of this paragraph uses a 20
point Times Roman italic font. The different fonts can
be seen with the View Document feature, but not in the
ordinary document screen.

1 100%   2 200%   3 Full Page   4 Facing Pages: 1   Doc 1 Pg 1

- *Figure 19.2: The document in Figure 19.1 as seen in the View Document Screen.*

Font selections made with either the Font command or the Format command override an initial base font selection made with the Print command.

Changing the Attributes of a Base Font

Once you have selected a base font, you may wish to modify a section of text with effects such as italics, boldface, or changes in point size. You can use the size and appearance features of the Font command to do this.

Size attributes

To change the size attribute of a section of text using the function key commands, press Ctrl-F8, select Size, then select the size you want from the resulting menu (see Table 19.1 below for more information about sizes). If you are using pull-down menus, open the Font menu and select the size you want from this menu. There are two ways to return to the base font. The easiest way is to press →. Alternately, you can press Ctrl-F8 (or open the Font menu) and then select Normal from the list of options. Selecting a size attribute places a pair of codes in your document (for example, [LARGE] and [large]) that mark the beginning and end of the section of text.

There are five available size attributes (and also superscripted and subscripted text options). When you select a size attribute, WordPerfect uses the font in your system that is closest in size to the size you selected. Table 19.1 shows how the size of these attributes compares to the current base font.

Size Attribute	Percentage of Base Font
Fine	60%
Small	80%
Large	120%
Very Large	150%
Extra Large	200%

Table 19.1: Size Attribute Ratios

Depending on your printer, you may also be able to change the appearance of your text using one of nine appearance attributes. These attributes are pictured in Figure 19.3. (The exact effect of appearance attributes varies from printer to printer.)

Appearance attributes

To change the appearance attribute for a section of text, press Ctrl-F8 (or open the Font menu), select Appearance, then select the appearance attribute you want. To return to the base font, you can either press → or you can press Ctrl-F8 (or open the Font menu) and select Normal. Selecting an appearance attribute places

Bold
Underline
Double Underline
Italic
Outline
Shadow
SMALL CAP
Redline
Strikeout

■ *Figure 19.3: The appearance attributes*

a pair of codes in your document (for example, **[ITALC]** and
[italc]) that mark the beginning and end of the section of text.

*Changing
attributes
in existing
text*

You can also change the size and/or appearance attributes in existing text. To do this, press Alt-F4 and move the cursor (or hold
down the left mouse button and drag the mouse) in order to highlight a section of text. With the Block On prompt still flashing,
press Ctrl-F8, select either Size or Appearance, and then select the
size or appearance attribute you want.

Merging Files

WordPerfect allows you to combine text from one file (the *primary* file) with data from a second file (the *secondary* file) in order to create multiple versions of the text file. In this Step, you will learn how to create primary and secondary files, and how to merge them to create form letters and mailing labels.

CREATING A SECONDARY FILE

The secondary files you use for merge operations contain carefully structured lists of data. You can create these files with WordPerfect, or you can import data files that you have created with other software programs. Secondary files are divided into parts known as *records* and *fields*. A record contains all the information about any one item in your list. Every record in a secondary file is divided into an equal number of fields, with each field containing a specific category of information about that record.

Secondary file structure

Figure 20.1 shows a data file that was created using WordPerfect. The file is divided into three records, with each record representing one person on the list. Each record consists of five fields. In this example, the fields contain the following information, in this order: last name, first name, title, job title, and department. Each field is numbered according to its position in the record. In this example, the last name field is Field 1, the first name field is Field 2, and so on.

Entering data into a secondary file

To create a secondary file using WordPerfect, begin with a clear document screen. Type in the information for the first field of the first record, then press F9 to mark the end of the field. This places an {END FIELD} marker at the end of the field and moves the cursor to a new line. (The {END FIELD} marker is equivalent to ^R in previous versions of WordPerfect.) Continue to enter data, pressing F9 at the end of each field, including the last field in the record. To mark the end of the record, press Shift-F9 (or open the Tools menu and select Merge Codes), and then select End Record. This places an {END RECORD} marker and a hard page break to mark the end of the record, and moves the cursor to the beginning of the next line, ready for the first field of the next record. (The {END RECORD} marker is equivalent to ^E in earlier versions of WordPerfect.) Place an {END RECORD} marker at the end of every record, including the last one in the data file.

Empty fields

If there are fields in your record for which you have no data, press F9 to place an {END FIELD} marker for those fields (see Field 4 in Record 3 of Figure 20.1, for example). This is important because fields are identified by their position in the record. If you omit any field, subsequent fields in that record will be incorrectly identified.

Create the data file shown in Figure 20.1, using the techniques just described. When you are done, save the file with the name

DATA. You will use this as a secondary file for creating form letters and mailing labels later in this Step.

CREATING A PRIMARY FILE

Primary merge files contain ordinary text interspersed with special merge codes. The merge codes determine where and how data from your secondary file is inserted into this document. Figure 20.2 shows an example of a primary merge file. The first merge code from this document is reproduced here:

```
{FIELD}2
```

When this document is merged with adata file, this code will be replaced by the data stored in the second field of each record. (The {FIELD} code is equivalent to ^F in earlier versions of WordPerfect.)

```
Chin{END FIELD}
Jerry{END FIELD}
Mr.{END FIELD}
Aquisitions Officer{END FIELD}
Aquisitions{END FIELD}
{END RECORD}
===========================================================================
Keenan{END FIELD}
Jennifer{END FIELD}
Miss{END FIELD}
Director{END FIELD}
Public Relations{END FIELD}
{END RECORD}
===========================================================================
Baker{END FIELD}
Lincoln{END FIELD}
Mr.{END FIELD}
{END FIELD}
Aquisitions{END FIELD}
{END RECORD}
===========================================================================


Field: 1                                    Doc 1 Pg 4 Ln 1" Pos 1"
```

- *Figure 20.1: A secondary merge file*

To place a {FIELD} code in a document, press Shift-F9, select Field, type the number that corresponds to the field you want to insert, and then press Enter.

Coding for blank fields

The code for Field 4 in Figure 20.2 has a question mark between the tilde (~) and the field number. This question mark tells WordPerfect not to print a blank line if the fourth field of a record contains no data. To add a question mark, insert a field code as described above, press ← once to move the cursor to the tilde, press ?, and then press → to move the cursor back to the end of the field code.

To create a sample primary file, work in the same directory you used when you created the data file, and begin with a clear document screen (F7, N, N). Create the document shown in Figure 20.2 as follows:

1. Insert the date as a code (Shift-F5, C), then press Enter twice.

```
February 19, 1992

{FIELD}2~ {FIELD}1~
{FIELD}4?~
{FIELD}5~

Dear {FIELD}3~ {FIELD}1~

Because of the recent educational crisis, federal funds for
defense spending have been severely curtailed.  We are planning a
flea market and bake sale to help raise funds locally.  We hope
you will be able to bring an item to sell.




C:\PRACTICE\MEMO                                    Doc 1 Pg 1 Ln 1" Pos 1"
```

■ *Figure 20.2: A primary merge file*

2. Press Shift-F9, select Field, type **2**, and then press Enter to insert the {FIELD}~2 marker.

3. Press the Spacebar to separate the first name from the last name, then insert the {FIELD}~1 marker (Shift-F9, F, 1, Enter).

4. Press Enter to move to a new line and insert a {FIELD}~4 marker (Shift-F9, F, 4, Enter). Press ← and type **?** to insert a question mark. Next, press → and then Enter to position the cursor for the next field.

5. Complete the memo as it appears in Figure 20.2, using the Shift-F9 command wherever you need to insert a {FIELD} code.

6. Save the completed document with the name MEMO.

MERGING FILES

When you merge files, you can either send output to the document screen and then print the results, or you can send the merged files directly to the printer. Merging to the document screen has the advantage of allowing you to proofread sample output before you print it; however, memory limitations may make it necessary to merge directly to the printer when you are working with a very large secondary file.

To merge to the document screen, begin with a clear document screen, then press Ctrl-F9 (or open the Tools menu) and select Merge. You will see the following prompt:

Merging to the document screen

```
Primary file:
```

Type the name of your primary file (the one with the document skeleton) and press Enter. (It may be necessary to type in the complete directory path as well as the file name.) This will result in the following prompt:

`Secondary file:`

Type in the name of your secondary file (the one with the data) and press Enter. You will see the following message while merging takes place:

`* Merging *`

When the merge operation is complete, the document screen will contain one copy of the primary document with the appropriate data from each record in your secondary file. WordPerfect automatically inserts a page break to separate each copy of the original document. To print the results, press Shift-F7 (or open the File menu and select Print) and select Full Document.

To merge the MEMO and DATA files you created earlier, begin with a clear document screen (F7, N, N), and proceed as follows:

1. Press Ctrl-F9 (or open the Tools menu) and select Merge.

2. Type **memo** in response to the first prompt.

3. Type **data** in response to the second prompt. When the merge is complete, you should have a three-page document on screen that contains one copy of the sample memo for each person in the data file.

4. Print the file (Shift-F7, F) and then clear the document screen without saving the merged output (F7, N, N).

Merging to the printer

To send the merged files directly to the printer, you must add two special merge codes, {PRINT} and {PAGE OFF}, to your primary merge file. The {PRINT} code sends the merged files directly to the printer, and the {PAGE OFF} code removes the hard returns that WordPerfect usually adds between copies of the original document during a merge. (If you don't insert this code, you will have an extra blank page between every copy of the document.)

To insert the {PRINT} and {PRINT OFF} codes, retrieve the primary merge file and move the cursor to the end of the document (Home, Home, ↓). Press Shift-F9 (or open the Tools menu and select Merge Codes) and select More. This will open a box containing a list of merge codes. (There are more merge codes than you can see at one time. You can scroll through this box using PgUp and PgDn, or you can press letters to move the cursor to different parts of the list.) Press **P**, use ↓ to highlight the {PRINT} code, and press Enter. This will insert a {PRINT} code at the end of the document. Insert a {PAGE OFF} code using this same technique. Save this updated version of your primary file (F10, Enter, Y), and then merge your primary file and secondary file following the directions above for merging to the document screen. You will see the * *Merging* * message on the status line while copies of your document are printed. (Press F1 to interrupt the merge process.)

CREATING MAILING LABELS

To create mailing labels, you must define a label style, create a master label document, and then use the Merge command to merge the master label document with your data file.

*Defining a
label style*

WordPerfect supplies you with a macro (LABELS.WPM) that you can use to define 19 different label styles. (It is also possible to define label styles using this keystroke sequence: Shift-F8, 2, 7, 5, 8, Y. Details of this technique are not covered in this book.) To use the label macro, press Alt-F10 (or open the Tools menu, select Macro, and select Execute), then type **labels** and press Enter. This will bring up an on-screen display that lists different label styles. (Press PgDn to see more styles and PgUp to return to the original list.) Highlight the style that matches your label sheets and press Enter. This will bring up a prompt that asks whether your labels will be fed continuously, from a separate bin, or manually. Choose the appropriate option (and respond to any additional questions if they appear as a result of your choice). When you are done, you should see the Format: Paper Size/Type screen. Select Exit from the menu at the bottom of this screen to complete the label definition. You will be returned to the document screen.

To practice with the label macro, select a two-column, 1" x 4" label format as follows: Press Alt-F10, type labels and press Enter, highlight definition B and press Enter, press C to select Continuous, and then press E to select Exit. You will use this label style later to print sample labels (on plain paper).

Creating a master label document

To create a master label document, use the same techniques you used to create a primary merge document, inserting {FIELD} markers where you want individual data items to appear on your labels.

To create a master label document, you can copy the first three lines of your memo document as directed below. (Both the Doc 1 and Doc 2 screens should be clear before you begin.)

1. Retrieve the MEMO document and move the cursor to the blank line under the date.

2. Press Alt-F4, then press ↓ four times to highlight the portion of the letter that contains the name, title, and department fields.

3. Press Ctrl-F4, select Block, and then select Copy to make a copy of the marked block.

4. Press Shift-F3 to change to the Doc 2 screen and press Enter to retrieve the block.

5. Save the document using the name MASTER.

6. Exit from Doc 2 (F7, N, Y) and then clear the Doc 1 screen (F7, N, N).

To complete the label-making process, merge your master label document with your data file using the technique described above for merging to the document screen. Once the merged results are on screen, you must change the current paper size and type to the label definition. To do this, move the cursor to the top of the merged file, press Shift-F8 (or open the Layout menu), select Page, select Paper Size/Type, highlight the label definition, press Enter, and then press F7 to return to the document screen. Once this is done, you can print the document.

Merging files to create labels

To print practice "labels" with the names in your DATA file, begin with a clear document screen, load your printer with ordinary paper, and proceed as follows:

1. Press Ctrl-F9, then select Merge.

2. Type **master** and press Enter in response to the primary file prompt.

3. Type **data** and press Enter in response to the secondary file prompt.

4. Press Home, Home, ↑ to move the cursor to the top of the merged document.

5. Press Shift-F8, select Page, and then select Paper Size/ Type to open the Format: Paper Size/Type menu.

6. Highlight the (1 x 4) label entry that you added to this list using the Label macro, and then press Enter to select this label format. Press F7 to return to the document screen.

7. Print the resulting document (Shift-F7, F). The three names should be arranged in two columns, as they would be on an actual label sheet.

8. Clear the screen without saving the merged document (F7, N, N).

IMPORTING DATA FROM OTHER SOURCES

Although you can create data files using WordPerfect, there are many other programs that are designed to simplify the creation and organization of database files. If your program can export files in *delimited DOS* format, you can use these files as secondary files to merge with WordPerfect primary files. A delimited DOS file stores data in ASCII text form with designated characters marking the divisions between fields and records. (For example, a comma might mark the end of each field and a carriage return the end of each record.) To use these files as secondary text files, you must tell WordPerfect what field and record delimiters are used. You can do this either during a merge operation, or you can give WordPerfect default settings for the delimiters in your data files.

To merge a delimited DOS text file, press Ctrl-F9 (or open the Tools menu) and select Merge, then enter the name of the primary file as usual. When you see the prompt for the secondary file, press Ctrl-F5. This will change the prompt to read *DOS Text Delimited File:*. Type the name (and path if necessary) of your data file and press Enter. This will display a screen that allows you to specify the delimiters that begin and end each field and record. (To enter a Line Feed command as a delimiter, press Enter. To enter a Carriage Return command as a delimiter, press Ctrl-M.) Once the delimiters are correctly entered, press Enter to complete the merge operation.

To change the default DOS text delimiters that WordPerfect recognizes, you can use the Setup menu. To do this, press Shift-F1 (or open the File menu and select Setup), select Initial Settings, and then select Merge. This will display the screen for specifying delimiters. Once you have entered the correct delimiters, press F7 to return to the document screen.

Index

* * * * * * * *

* (asterisk)
    to mark fonts, 138
    to mark List Files screen, 31
    in Spell Check lookup
        feature, 88
[] (square brackets) for hidden
    codes, 48
[/] Cancel Hyphenation code, 108
+ (plus sign) for marking fonts, 138
? (question mark)
    for blank fields in merge file, 148
    in Spell Check lookup feature, 88

A

absolute tabs, 62
adjective lists in Thesaurus, 92
Alt-= key combination to open menu
    bar, 9
Alt-key combination macros, 128
    executing, 130,–131
antonym list in Thesaurus, 92
appearance attributes of font,
    143–144
Append (Move command) for text
    block, 71, 72
*Are other copies of WordPerfect
currently running?* prompt, 122
asterisk (*)
    to mark fonts, 138
    to mark List Files screen, 31
    in Spell Check lookup feature, 88
AUTOEXEC.BAT file, 2, 3
    mouse driver in, 4

B

backup copies, 31–32
    automatic, options for, 121–123
backward search, 78–79

Base Font, 136
    attributes of, 142–144
    changing, 139–142
.BK! file name extension, 122
Block command, 69–73
Block Copy command for headers
    and footers, 101
Block Protect feature, 96
    for parallel columns, 111
blocks of text, 69–76
    deleting, 72
    font attributes for, 144
    marking, 69–70
    preventing page break within, 96
    retrieving, 72
    saving as file, 72
    text enhancements for, 72–73
boldface text, 41–42
    for block, 72
bottom margins, 57
    footer placement and, 102
bullet in Thesaurus list, 92

C

Cancel Hyphenation code [/], 108
Cancel key (F1), 9
    to close menu without changes, 12
    function of, 21–22
    for restoring deleted text, 21
    for restoring hidden codes, 52
capitalization, spell check of, 90
Caps Lock key, 8
carriage return, 17
    as delimiter, 154
cartridge fonts, 135
case sensitivity
    in Replace command, 84
    in searches, 80

Center command (Shift-F6) for
  header and footer position, 100
center justification, 58
center tabs, 63
centering text, 42–43
centimeters, 120
clearing screen display, 26–27
columns, 109–116
  and cursor movement, 116
  defining format for, 109–110
  distance between, 112
  manually setting margins for, 113
  selecting type, 110–112
  setting number of, 112
  strategies for using, 114–116
  turning on and off, 113–114
commands, canceling, 9
compressed archived files, 2
CONFIG.SYS file, 2
confirmation in Replace command,
  82–84
Copy (Move command) for text
  block, 71
copying files in List Files
  command, 31
cpi (characters per inch), 136
Ctrl-B (^B) for page number in
header text, 100
Ctrl-End (Delete to End of Line
command), 63
Ctrl-X (^X) symbol for wildcard
search, 80
cursor
  location of, 6–7
  mouse, 10
  in Reveal Codes display, 50
cursor movement, 18–20
  columns and, 116
  and initial margin codes, 57

D

dates, entering in document, 126–127
decimal tabs, 63–64
default settings, 117–124
  automatic file backup, 121–123
  directory, 30
  Escape repetition number, 126
  left margin, 7
  menus, 118–119
  page-formatting features, 117–118
  units of measure, 119–120
Delete (Del) key, 20
Delete (Move command) for text
  block, 71
Delete to End of Line command
(Ctrl-End), 63
deleting
  blocks of text, 72
  hidden codes, 50
  macros, 131
  tab settings, 63
  text and restoring, 20-n-22
delimited DOS format, 154
dictionaries, 89
  supplemental, 85
directories
  changing, 12–13
  choosing, 30
  creating for files, 5–6
  for macro files, 131
  for soft fonts, 137
  for temporary backup files, 122
Doc indicator, 6–7
document screen, printing from,
  33–34
Document to be saved: prompt, 23, 25
Document to be retrieved prompt, 27
documents
  multiple-page, 95–102

switching between, 32
DOS (Disk Operating System), 1
DOS commands, MD (make
   directory), 6
dot leaders, 64–65
double words, spell checker search
   for, 89–90
downloading fonts, 136
drives, retrieving files from
   different, 32

E

Edit menu
   for manipulating text block, 71
   Reveal Codes, 48
   Switch Document, 32
   Undelete, 21
editing, 17–22
   hyphenation, 107–108
{END FIELD}, 146
{END RECORD}, 146
Esc key for repeating keystrokes,
   125–126
Exit key (F7), 100
exiting WordPerfect, 15
   saving files when, 26

F

{FIELD}, 147–148
fields, 145
file name extensions
   .BK!, 122
   .WPM, 131
File menu
   Exit, 15
   List Files, 28–29
   Print, Full Document option, 33
   Retrieve, 27
   Setup, 105–106

Setup, Environment, Units of
Measure, 119
   Setup, Initial Codes, 117
   Setup, Location of Files, 122
files
   adding text block to different, 71
   combining, 29
   compressed archived, 2
   copying, 31
   creating directory for, 5–6
   inserting additional file in current,
      27, 29
   for macros, 131
   merging, 145–155
   retrieving, 27–30
   saving and naming for first time,
      23–24
   saving block of text as, 72
   saving updated, 24–25
flashing *Pos* indicator, 8
floppy disks, copying back-up files
   to, 31–32
Flush Right command (Alt-F6) for
header and footer position, 100
font cartridges, installing, 136–137
Font command, 140
fonts, 135–144
   adding, 135–136
   selecting, 139–142
footers, 98–102
   editing existing, 101
   placement on page, 102
Format command, selecting Base
Font using, 140–142
Format menu
   Line, 43, 56
   Line, Justification, 58
   Line, Tab Set, 61
   Page, 57
   Page, Headers and footers, 99

Suppress, 98
formatting codes. *See* hidden codes
Forward (Search menu), 78
full justification, 58
function keys, 8–9
  Cancel (F1), 21–22
  Exit (F7), 15
  Help (F3), 13–14
  Left Indent (F4), 59
  List Files (F5), 28–29
  Underline (F8), 42

G

graphic display of printed
  document, 36
graphics, printing only, 39
Graphics Quality option (Print
  menu), 39

H

hard disk drive, 1
hard hyphens, 106
hard page command (Ctrl-Enter), 95
  to begin new column, 115
hard return, 17
hardware requirements, 1–2
headers, 98–102
  editing, 101
  placement on page, 102
headwords, 92
help, online, 13–14
hidden codes, 42
  for columns, 114
  deleting, 50
  for indentation, 59
  for margins, 56, 57
  for page numbering, 97
  restoring deleted, 52
  search for, 77, 80–82

for tabs, 65
viewing, 47–54
[HRt] code, 49, 51
hyphenation, 103–108
  editing, 107–108
  prompt for, 104–106
  turning on and off, 103–104
hyphens, types of, 106–107

I

importing data for secondary merge
  files, 154
indented paragraphs, 59–60
Initial Base Font, 141
initializing printer, 138, 139
Insert (Ins) key, 22
insert mode, 22
inserting text, 22
installing
  font cartridges, 136–137
  mouse, 4
  soft fonts, 137–139
  WordPerfect, 1–4
invisible soft returns, 107
Irregular Case menu (spell check), 90

J

justification style for margins, 58–60

K

keyboard
  for cursor movement, 18–19
  for cursor movement through
    columns, 116
  to mark text block, 69–70
  for menu selection, 12
keystrokes, Esc key for repeating,
  125–126

L

LABELS.WPM macro file, 151–152
Layout menu
  Align, Indent ->, 59
  Line, Hyphenation, 103
  Page, 57
Left and Right Indent command
  (Shift-F4), 59
Left Indent command (F4), 59
left justification, 58
left margins, 56
  default setting for, 7
left tabs, 63
Line Feed command as
  delimiter, 154
line spacing, 43–44
List Files command (F5), 28–29
  changing directory in, 30
  Copy feature, 31
  Other Directory option, 12–13
  Print, 34–35
Ln indicator, 7
Look Up option in spelling feature, 88

M

Macro Define command,
  canceling, 129
macros, 127–134
  to define label styles, 151–152
  defining, 128–130
  deleting, 131
  executing, 130–131
  files for, 131
  pausing for input, 132–134
mailing labels from merge files,
  151–154
margins, 55–57
  changing defaults for, 117

header and footer placement
  and, 102
  justification style for, 58–60
  setting manually for columns, 113
  tabs and, 62–63
marking blocks of text, 69–70
MD (make directory) command, 6
measurement units
  default settings for, 119–120
  for margins, 55
memory-resident software, 2
menu bar, Alt-= to open, 9
menus, 12
  changing options for, 118–119
  closing without changes, 12
  using mouse with, 11
merge codes, 146
  in primary merge file, 147
merging files, 145–155
  to create mailing labels, 151–154
  process for, 149–151
mouse
  for cursor movement, 20
  for giving commands, 10–12
  installing, 4
  to mark text block, 70
  menu for, 123–124
  for menu selection, 12
mouse cursor, 10
mouse driver, 4, 124
Mouse type menu (Set-up), 4
Move command (Ctrl-F4), 70–71
multiple copies, printing, 38
multiple documents
  working with, 32
  printing, 35
multiple files, copying, 31
multiple-page documents, 95–102

N

names for macros, 128
newspaper columns, 110
Num Lock key, 8
numeric keypad, 19

O

online help, 13–14
Original Document Backup option,
    122–123

P

page breaks, 95–96
page numbers, 96–98
    suppressing, 98
    turning off, 98
{PAGE OFF} merge code, 150–151
pages
    changing initial formatting
        features, 117–118
    graphic view of layout, 37
    printing selected, 38
    shortcuts for working with, 73–74
paired hidden codes, deleting, 51
paragraphs
    indented, 59–60
    shortcuts for working with, 73–74
parallel columns, 110–111
    text entry in, 115–116
path, 24
pause in macros, 132–134
Pg indicator, 7
plus sign (+) for marking fonts, 138
points, 120, 136
Pos (position) indicator, 7–8, 66
    boldface and, 42
primary merge file, 145
    creating, 147–149

Print command
    Select Printer, Edit, Initial Base
Font, 141–142
    View Document feature, 35–37
{PRINT} merge code, 150–151
printer
    initializing, 138, 139
    merging files directly to, 150–151
    selecting in INSTALL program, 3
    and smallest permitted margin, 56
printing, 33–39
    control options for, 37–39
    controlling quality of, 39
    from document screen, 33–34
    from List Files screen, 34–35
    multiple copies, 38
    multiple documents, 35
    only text or only graphics, 39
prompts, 6
    *Are other copies of WordPerfect
        currently running?*, 122
    Document to be saved:, 23, 25
    Document to be retrieved, 27
    *Retrieve into current
        document?*, 29
pull-down menus, 9–10
    displaying, 118–119

Q

question mark (?)
    for blank fields in merge file, 148
    in Spell Check lookup feature, 88

R

RAM (random access memory), 1
records, 145
relative tabs, 62
Replace command, 82–84
resident fonts, 135

restoring deleted text, 21
retrieval of files, 27–30
Retrieve into current document
  prompt, 29
returns, hard and soft, 17
Reveal Codes command, 47–54
  display for, 47–48
  editing with screen visible, 50–52
right justification, 58
right margins, 56
right tabs, 63

S

save process
  when exiting WordPerfect, 26
  for file, 23–24
  for text block as file, 72
  for updated files, 24–25
scalable fonts, 136, 140
screen display
  clearing, 26–27
  double dashed line on, for page
break, 95
  merging to, 149–150
  for Reveal Codes command, 47–48
  scrolling, 19
  for Thesaurus, 92
scrolling, 19
Search command, 77–82
  for hidden codes, 80–82
search and replace, 77–84
  case sensitivity in, 80
  changing direction of, 79
search string, 78
  wildcard characters in, 80
secondary merge file, 145
  creating, 145–147
  importing data for, 154

sentences, shortcuts for working
  with, 73–74
serial mouse port, 124
Setup menu, 117–124
  Backup, 121
  hyphenation prompt frequency in,
    105–106
  Location of Files, 131
  mouse, 123–124
single spacing, 43
size attribute of font, 142–143
soft fonts, 135–136
  installing, 137–139
soft hyphens, 106
soft page code, 95
  for column breaks, 115
soft return, 17
  invisible, 107
Spell screen, menu options in, 87
spell check, 85–90
  interrupting, 86
  Look Up feature in, 88
  special features of, 89–90
square brackets ([ ]) for hidden
  codes, 48
[SRt] code, 49
starting WordPerfect, 6
status line, 6
supplemental dictionary, 85
switching between documents, 32
synonyms, 91

T

[Tab] code, 49, 51
tab ruler line, 61
tabs, 61–67
  changing defaults for, 117
  deleting existing, 63

setting at uniform intervals, 65
setting new, 63–65
types of, 62–63
temporary files for timed backup, 121
text. *See also* blocks of text
   adding columns to existing, 115
   deletion of, 20–22
   inserting, 22
   printing only, 39
   restoring deleted, 21
   search for, 79–80
text enhancements, 41–46. *See also*
   hidden codes
   boldface, 41–42
   centering, 42–43
   deleting, 50–51
   for text block, 72–73
   underlining, 42
Text Column Definition menu,
   109–110
Text Quality option (Print menu), 39
(Text was not modified) message, 26
thesaurus, 91–93
Timed Document Backup option, 121
Tools menu
   Macro, Define, 128
   Merge Codes, 141
   Spell, 85–88
   Thesaurus, 91
top margins, 7, 57
   header placement and, 102

typeover mode, 22

U

underlining, 42
units of measurement
   default settings for, 119–120
   for margins, 55
updated files, saving, 24–25
user interface, 5–15

V

View Document feature (Print menu),
   35–37
   justification style on, 59
   to see fonts, 140

W

wildcard characters in search
   string, 80
WordPerfect
   exiting, 15
   installing, 1–4
   saving files when exiting, 26
   starting, 6
WordPerfect 4.2 units, 120
.WPM file name extension, 131
WP{WP}.BK1 file, 121–122
WP{WP}.BK2 file, 121–122
WP{WP}US.LEX dictionary file, 89
WP{WP}US.SUP dictionary file, 89